This collection of stories, poems and illustrations celebrates Book Aid International's fiftieth birthday. Over the years we have provided more than twenty-one million books to children and adults in some of the world's poorest countries. Each book is placed in a library or a school so it can be read over and over again and help to educate many people.

Sadly there are more than 100 million children in the world today who don't have the chance to go to school. But each year this number gets a little less as more schools are built and free education is offered in more and more countries. Every single one of these children needs books so that they can learn to read; so we still have a huge job to do.

Thank you for helping us by buying this book!

We hope that you enjoy reading the wonderful stories in this book. We want all children, everywhere, to be able to share this simple pleasure.

Please take a look at our web site to find out more: www.bookaid.org

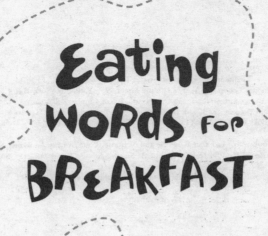

Eating WORDS FOR BREAKFAST

BOOK AID INTERNATIONAL

PUFFIN BOOKS

Published by the Penguin Group
Penguin Books Ltd, 80 Strand, London WC2R 0RL, England
Penguin Group (USA), 375 Hudson Street, New York, New York 10014, USA
Penguin Books Australia Ltd, 250 Camberwell Road, Camberwell, Victoria 3124, Australia
Penguin Books Canada Ltd, 10 Alcorn Avenue, Toronto, Ontario, Canada M4V 3B2
Penguin Books India (P) Ltd, 11 Community Centre, Panchsheel Park, New Delhi – 110 017,
India
Penguin Books (NZ) Ltd, Cnr Rosedale and Airborne Roads, Albany, Auckland, New Zealand
Penguin Books (South Africa) (Pty) Ltd, 24 Sturdee Avenue, Rosebank 2196, South Africa

Penguin Books Ltd, Registered Offices: 80 Strand, London WC2R 0RL, England

www.penguin.com

First published 2004

1

Set in Bembo 12pt

Made and printed in England by Clays Ltd, St Ives plc

British Library Cataloguing in Publication Data
A CIP catalogue record for this book is available from the British Library

ISBN 0–141–31767–1

Eating Words for Breakfast

BOOK AID INTERNATIONAL

PUFFIN

Contents

Title page illustration by Kate Cadbury

Shirley Hughes

Foreword

I've been hooked on reading ever since I was six years old. I read voraciously throughout my childhood. I might have looked as if I was simply curled up in an armchair but I was really climbing the Faraway Tree, hunting Heffalumps with Pooh and Piglet, turning topsy-turvy with Mary Poppins, dancing with Pauline Petrova and Posy, and skating across thin ice with Jo and Amy.

I had a perfectly ordinary bread-and-butter boring childhood but, through books, I starved with Oliver Twist, suffered at school with Jane Eyre and hid in an attic with Anne Frank.

I'd never been further than Clacton-on-Sea for a week's holiday, but by reading I sailed to deserted islands with Robinson Crusoe, I flew to Never-never land with Peter Pan and Wendy and I whirled up in a twister all the way to Oz. There didn't seem so many stories way back then about children living all over the *real* world. I did run barefoot in the Swiss Alps with Heidi but that was about it.

It's wonderful that British children now read about life all over the world. There are stories in this super anthology from Palestine, Zimbabwe, Uganda, Ghana and Nigeria – plus contributions from some of the UK's best loved authors and illustrators. The stories, poems and pictures are immensely varied, but they open up new worlds and show us a glimpse of all sorts of other lives. Every writer and illustrator has given their work for free so that all the money raised will help Book Aid International provide books for children and adults around the world. BAI provides three-quarters of a million books every year to people who would otherwise have no access to vital books or information.

I find it so moving that this charity recognizes the need for books in deprived communities. They offer solace, stimulation, entertainment, escape and education – true food for the soul.

I hope everyone enjoys the fantastic stories, poems and artwork in this anthology as much as I have. Happy reading!

Jacqueline Wilson
(UNITED KINGDOM)
Illustrated by Shirley Hughes

Satellite Batteries

by Eoin Colfer
(IRELAND)

illustrated by Guy Parker-Rees

Gerry sat on JJ's window sill with his head in his hands. It was no use. You could only search your pockets so many times. The money was gone; he'd lost it. There was no point in retracing his steps, either. English Ned had already made two sweeps of the street before shuffling down to the off-licence. Nope, if the cash had slipped out of Gerry's pocket, it had long since been converted into cider.

Things wouldn't have been so bad if it'd been his own money. Gerry snorted. Chance would be a fine thing. When was the last time he'd had his own money? But it was Dad's cigarette money. And cigarettes were important to Dad. Since his back had given out, Dad said a nice fag with a cup of tea was one of the few pleasures he had left.

'Those fags will kill you,' Gerry had said.

Tom Coghlan had smiled a sad smile and said, 'They'll never get the chance, son.'

Gerry didn't like it when his dad talked like that.

Some shopkeepers would let you put things on account until pay day, but not JJ Foley. JJ didn't believe in accounts. He always said that an account was a temptation for the weak and penniless. Bit of an old Scrooge, was JJ; not exactly brimming over with the milk of human kindness. His white shop-coat was smeared with the stains of a decade. The under-tens believed that those stains were the blood and brains of shoplifters that JJ had dragged into the back room. Gerry knew better. He knew better, but he didn't believe it.

JJ had a big bullfrog lump on his neck, too. It was impossible not to stare at it, but if you were caught, it meant a lifetime ban from Foley's. Then you'd have to walk all the way downtown for your shopping, with the wind from the quay taking the skin off your face.

'Hey, Coghlan! Get off my window.'

Gerry didn't even have to look. This window sill belonged to Bobby Mac and the tracksuit brigade. They congregated here every weekend to share cigarettes and scratch their initials with spent matches. Usually Gerry would have moved on, but today ... today the world was closing in on him.

'I told you to get off my window.'

Funny: all your life you go around avoiding fights like the plague, terrified of the pain they bring; then one day, for some reason, a fight seems like the best thing in the world.

Bobby Mac didn't know this. He thought today was

just like every other day of his short, mean life.

'Your precious dad isn't here to fight your battles today, Coghlan.'

Gerry lifted his face from his hands. He stood up slowly, feeling taller than his five foot two. As usual, Bobby had new clothes on. All the latest.

'And your gang aren't here either, Mac.'

'So?'

'So I might have to dirty your precious rap-star tracksuit if you say one more word about my dad.'

The tracksuit jibe hit home. Bullies are vain by nature.

'You watch what you're saying!'

But Gerry was in no mood to watch anything. Bobby Mac had been at him since High Babies. Seven years of dead arms and teasing. Enough was enough.

'My dad's been teaching me how to box. So I can take you on. My mam will hammer your parents, and my dad can be a spare.'

Mac was disgusted. His belly shook like a slab of lard. 'You just –'

Gerry went nose to nose with him. 'What?'

'What yourself?'

That was only baby talk, so Gerry decided to throw in a few more insults.

'I don't know why you love yourself so much, Bobby – that's a girl's name, by the way – because you're only a fat eejit dressed up like some American gom.'

Gerry took a surprised breath. He couldn't believe

those words had made the journey from his brain to his mouth.

'Well, at least I have clothes,' countered Bobby. Not the best line in the world.

'So have I.'

'Yeah. Knacker's clothes.'

'I'd rather have knacker's clothes than some stupid fashion-victim get-up. You're only a nerd trying to be cool.'

'At least my dad can buy me proper clothes. He has a job. He doesn't sit at home all day, scratching his bum and watching oul' ones' programmes on the TV.'

'Your dad can have all the jobs he wants, he could be the president of the world, and he'd still be a thick eejit. And your ma can dress you up like a fairy all year and it won't put any brains in your head!'

'Fairy? Fairy!' Bobby wasn't calling Gerry a fairy. He was just repeating it to make sure he'd heard it. 'Aaargh!'

Gerry laughed. Who wouldn't?

'Go on with your "aaargh". Is that one of those rap words?'

So then Gerry had his first real fight. He'd often been in fights before, but never in one where he'd fought back.

Mac charged, his arms pinwheeling. Gerry noticed that his eyes were closed. It was funny, really, so Gerry chanced a giggle. He stopped sharpish when one of the rotating fists connected with his lip.

The old impulse surfaced then: lie down and weather

the storm. But not today. Gerry picked his target and thumped Mac right in the wobbling belly. The bully's breath escaped in a shower of spittle, and he collapsed among the sweet papers and chewing-gum patties.

Gerry's triumph was cut short by the sight of strings of blood swinging from his own mouth. He sank into his earned place on the window sill and dabbed at his war wound with an unravelling sleeve.

After a minute or so, Mac struggled up beside him. He'd stopped whooping, but there wasn't a shade of colour in his cheeks.

'Do you really not like my clothes, Coghlan?'

Gerry shrugged. Bobby Mac had been mean to him his whole life. Because of Bobby Mac, he hated going to school. Because of Bobby Mac, he had no friends. But Gerry wasn't Bobby Mac. His point had been proved.

'No, they're grand. Not my style, but grand. I was just scoring points.'

Mac nodded. 'I didn't mean it about your dad, either. About the oul' one's TV and everything.'

Gerry nodded. This was unexpected.

And it wasn't over yet. 'You can sit on my window sill if you like. Just until the boys get here, though. One step at a time.'

Gerry had to laugh. 'That's right, Bobby boy. One step at a time.'

They were quiet for a minute then, a bit uneasy with this new alliance.

'So what's the problem?' asked Mac at last. 'You were in a bit of a state when I came over.'

Gerry took a deep breath.

'I lost my dad's cigarette money.'

'So?'

'So I can't go home without those cigarettes. Dad's fed up enough without this.'

Bobby stood up, wiping the dirt from the seat of his shiny tracksuit. 'No problem. We'll rob the fags.'

'Rob? What about JJ?'

Bobby laughed, a little sneery laugh. Apparently even a box in the gullet couldn't knock the cockiness out of this fellow.

'That old eejit! He's blind as a bat. I'm always lifting stuff here.'

'But —'

'Gerry. Are we friends now or what? Trust me, will you?'

Gerry didn't know. He couldn't get that stained shop-coat out of his head. He knew for sure that one fellow who'd escaped from JJ's back room had gone straight to the Rosslare ferry, without even saying goodbye to his family.

'Yeah, but stealing...'

But Gerry's objections sounded lame even to himself – lame and chicken; and anyway, Bobby Mac was gone. In through the *Star Trek* whoosh doors, bold as brass. Gerry hurried after him, afraid that if the doors closed he would be shut out of this new world forever.

JJ stood behind the counter, with a fresh stain on his shop-coat. It was green and Italy-shaped. Gerry wondered what colour brains were. The shopkeeper's neck-lump was just hanging there, like a brown hot-water bottle, wobbling a bit with each breath. The boys tried not to stare, but it was hypnotic.

'Morning, gents.' JJ called all males 'gents'.

'Morning, JJ,' answered Mac jauntily.

Gerry nodded, too scared to talk.

'What can I do you for?' JJ's little joke. The same joke, every day. Yawn.

Mac scratched his chin, like he was thinking about it. 'I need a battery for the satellite remote. A small one.'

JJ frowned. He loved a retail challenge.

'Pencil, like for a Walkman?'

'No, smaller.'

'The little stubby ones?'

'No. Small and thin.'

Now it was JJ's turn to scratch. Gently, along the line of his lump.

'I might have some in the store. Hang on.'

He disappeared behind the freezer into the back room.

'Sucker,' gloated Mac. He skirted the counter to the till area. 'Will a hundred do you?'

Gerry nodded dumbly. A hundred. So easy. All his life, he'd been paying for things.

Mac grabbed stacks of cigarettes from the shelf, stuffing them down the back of his tracksuit. It looked like he had a square behind. Robot bum.

'Didn't I tell you? A cinch. That JJ is an awful eejit. Batteries for the satellite ... I just made that up, you know.'

Gerry's smile widened. He could go behind there too. Why not? A bar of chocolate would be nice – and maybe a few cans of cola, too ...

He had taken one step, just one, when JJ jumped out from behind the fridge and grabbed Mac by the scruff of the neck.

'Eejit, am I? I'll give you eejit!'

We're caught, thought Gerry. No cigarettes, and no life.

'Satellite batteries! I'll give you satellite batteries!'

Gerry didn't think that JJ was actually going to give them satellite batteries.

'I have you this time, Bobby Mac!'

Bobby started squealing. He sounded more like a wounded piglet than a trendy rap-star clone. 'Let go of me! Let go!'

'You won't talk your way outta this one.' JJ's lump was pumping up like a balloon.

'I'll tell Dada!'

Dada? Another time, another place, there would be tears of laughter for sure.

'Don't worry, you little reprobate. I'll be telling him for you. Thought I'd run off into the store for your batteries, didn't you? Well, not this time, mister. Once bitten is enough for me!'

Bobby cracked. Gerry could see it coming in the slyness of his eyes.

'Gerry Coghlan made me take them. He made me.'

Friends. I'll be there for youuu ... Maybe not.

JJ looked so mad his eyebrows met in the middle.

'Gerry Coghlan? Gerry Coghlan? Everyone knows the Coghlans are as honest as the day is long. You've sunk to a new low this time – blaming others for your own mischief.'

'But –'

'Never mind your buts. I don't see any cigarettes shoved down the back of Gerry's trousers!'

'He made me, I'm telling you. He made me!'

But JJ wasn't having any of it. 'Oh, shut up with your squealing. You're embarrassing yourself. It's the back room for you until the guards get here.'

He dragged Mac off, kicking and screaming, heels dragging skidmarks along the lino. A new stain for the coat. Not that Gerry would miss him. They hadn't been buddies long.

Gerry spotted something on the floor: a golden cuboid. Twenty cigarettes had shimmied down Mac's pants. There on the floor, salvation. He saw his fingers reaching for the cigarettes, saw them curling around the box ... They were his. He shoved the box down his jumper.

'Gerry?'

It was JJ. The jailer was back. Gerry tried to spot any new stains; it helped him to not look at the lump.

'Yes?'

'Sorry about that Bobby Mac. He's an awful case.'

Gerry grinned weakly. 'I blame the parents.'

JJ grinned back. 'And do you know what? You'd be dead right.'

He reached into the cooler and pulled out a can of cola. 'There you are, young fella. That's for being one of the few honest customers I have left.'

Gerry could feel the cigarette box cutting into his stomach.

'Thanks, JJ.'

'What did you want, anyway?'

Good question.

'Em ... a can of cola. But, sure, I can save my money now.'

JJ chuckled. 'That's right. Good lad. You better run along now, before that chap's dada gets here. There's going to be a whole heap of shouting.'

'OK, JJ. See you later.'

Gerry sidled towards the door with his can. He popped the top and drank deeply. JJ had his back to him, already roaring into the phone. No prizes for guessing who was at the other end.

Everything was perfect. Mac was being punished, Dad's fags were tucked into his waistband, and he even had a can of cola to himself – no brothers or sisters looking for slobbery sups – as a bonus. Not to mention the satisfaction of punching Mac right in the flabby gut.

But JJ looked different to him now. He wasn't a monster any more; he was just a fellow trying to hold on to his livelihood, keeping the wolf from the door. Like Gerry's own dad had been, before his back gave out.

'I'm afraid not,' JJ was saying, making no attempt to soften the blow. 'It was your boy all right ... He's the ringleader ... Caught him red-handed ... Yell all you like; it's the guards' affair now. So you'd better stop making excuses and get down here before they drag him off in the squad car ... '

It went on like that: threat and counter-threat, just like Gerry and Mac. Some things never changed.

Gerry took a step towards freedom. The sensor picked it up and activated the doors – whoosh. They waited expectantly. One more step and he'd be out in the wide world, away with his ill-gotten gains – cigarettes and cola, plus the memory of that punch.

One more step. One leg in front of the other ...

But he couldn't do it. There was too much of his dad in him.

Gerry shook the cigarette box out of his waistband. It plopped down on to the lino, by the toe of his boot. JJ didn't see a thing; he was still shouting into the phone.

Phase two of the plan was to slide the box towards the counter where he'd picked it up. It was difficult to judge; the surface was uneven, and dried puddles could slow the missile down.

Gerry chose a side-footer, sending the cigarettes

spinning down the length of the shop – spinning too fast, as it happened. They were going to whack into the base of the counter.

The cola saved him. He covered the impact with a huge burp.

''Scuse me,' he muttered hopefully.

JJ waved him away, far too deep in his argument to be concerned with Gerry's pipes.

The next step in Operation Confession would logically be to march up to the counter and admit his part in the larceny. But, Gerry thought as the *Star Trek* doors closed behind him, in the words of Bobby Mac: one step at a time.

For the first time in his life, Gerry Coghlan couldn't wait for school on Monday.

Bobby Mac. Dada. Oh, the possibilities …

The Beastman of Ballyloch

by Michael Morpurgo
(UNITED KINGDOM)

illustrated by Michael Foreman

There was once an ogre so pitted and crumpled in his face, so twisted in his body, that no one could bear to even look at him. He was known in all the country around as 'The Beastman of Ballyloch'. He lived by himself on a small island in the middle of a great dark lake. Being left on his own as a small child, as he had when his mother died, and shunned ever since by all humankind, he had never learned to speak as other men do, so that when he tried he sounded like a cawing, croaking crow, and no words came out.

Lonely though he was on his island, he was never completely alone, for with him lived all the wild things he loved so well – the squirrels, the otters, the herons and the moorhens. But of all the creatures that lived with him on the island, it was the swans he loved best. He mended their broken wings, untangled them from fishing twine and drove the marauding gulls away from their nests. For the swans, the island was a safe haven. They knew the ogre was not like the people who lived across the lake in the village of Ballyloch. He would not hurt them or steal their eggs, or throw sticks at them. To them, he was not at all hideous. He was their guardian and the kindest man that ever lived, a trusted friend.

He lived simply in the log cabin he had built for himself, under a thatched roof he had thatched himself. Under the thatch it was cool enough in the summer months and, just so long as he kept the fire going, warm enough in the winter too. He grew all the corn he needed in his one-acre field, and all the vegetables he could want in the sheltered garden behind the log cabin. When the fish were rising of an evening in the great dark lake, then he would often go out in his boat and catch himself a fine fish for his supper – sea trout perhaps, or brown trout, or even better a silver salmon fresh up from the sea. The ogre needed to eat well, for he was half as big again as any man in Ballyloch.

Much as the people of Ballyloch hated the sight of the ogre, they needed him, for he was the best thatcher for miles around and they knew it. He was also the cheapest. All he asked in payment for a day's work was a wheelbarrow of peat for his fire. So whenever there was a barn or a house to be rethatched, he would set out across the lake in his boat, and he would always be escorted by a flotilla of swans. The villagers would see him coming, and the cry would go up. 'The Beastman is coming! The Beastman is coming!' Many of the children would be hustled away indoors as he tied up his boat by the quayside, and as he came limping up the village street. Others, the older ones more often, would laugh and jeer at him, throw stones at him even; then run off screaming up the alleyways. He did not blame them. He had ears. He knew well enough what they had been told: 'Don't you ever go near the Beastman. He's mad. He's bad. Don't ever set foot on his island either. If you do he'll gobble you up.'

In spite of this, the ogre did his best to smile at everyone. He would always wave cheerily, but not one of them would ever wave back nor greet him kindly. The ogre endured all the averted eyes, all the wicked whisperings, all the children's taunts because he loved to be amongst his own, to hear the sound of human voices, to see the people at their work, the children at their play, to feel that he was once more a man amongst men. From high up on a rooftop, as he drove in his spars or combed his thatch, he could look down on the village and watch them all go about their lives. That was as close as he was ever going to get to them. He knew he could hope for nothing more. In all his life he had never once been invited into their houses, never once warmed himself at their hearths. He would do his day's thatching, wheel his barrowload of peat down to the quayside in the evening, load his boat and row back to his island across the great dark lake, his beloved swans swimming alongside.

It was a summer's day and there was a fresh run of sea trout in the lake. Dozens of fishing boats had come out from Ballyloch, and the sound of happy children rippled across the water. The ogre sat on the grassy bank of his island and watched them. He thought at first it was the sound of flying swans, their wings singing in the air, but then he saw her, a young woman in a straw hat. It was she who was singing. She was standing up in her boat and hauling in her line. Her boat was close to the island, closer to the shore than they usually came, much closer than all the other boats. How the ogre's heart soared as he listened. Nothing was ever as sweet as this.

There was a sudden shriek and splash, and the boat was empty and rocking violently. The straw hat was floating on the water, but of the young woman there was no sign at all. The ogre did not stop even to take off his boots and his jacket. He dived straight into the icy water and swam out towards the boat. He saw her come up once, her hands clutching at the air before she sank again. She came up a second time, gasping for life, and was down again almost at once. The ogre went after her, caught her round the waist and brought her to the surface. He swam her back to the island and laid her down in the grass. She lay there, limp and lifeless, not a movement, not a breath. The ogre called and called to her, but she would not wake. He held his head in his hands and wept out loud.

'Why are you crying?' She was speaking! The ogre took his hands away. She was sitting up! 'You're the Beastman, aren't you?' she went on, shrinking from him.

She looked around her. 'I'm on the island, aren't I? I shouldn't be here. I shouldn't be talking to you.' For a few moments she stared at him and said nothing. 'It must have been you that saved me. You pulled me out!' The ogre thought of speaking, but dared not. The sound of his croaking voice would only make him more fearsome, more repellent. The girl was suddenly smiling at him. 'You did, didn't you? You saved my life. But why? After all I did to you. When I was a child I used to throw stones at you, do you know that? I used to laugh at you. And now you've saved my life.'

The ogre had to speak, had to tell her none of that mattered, had to tell her how beautifully she sang. He tried, but of course all that came out was a crow's croak. 'All right,' she went on. 'Maybe you can't speak words, but you can speak. And you can hear me, can't you? My father — you know my father. He's the weaver. You thatched our house once when I was little, remember? He always told me you were bad. But you're not, are you? He said you were mad too, that you gobble up little children for your tea. But you're not like that at all. I know from your eyes you're not. How can I ever thank you? I have nothing to give you. I am not rich. I know, I know. Shall I teach you to speak words? Shall I? First I shall teach you my name — Miranda. Miranda. You will say it. You will.' The ogre took her small hands in his and wept again, but this time for sheer joy. 'And I'm going to tell everyone what you did, and they won't ever believe any more all the horrible things they've heard about you.' She shivered suddenly. 'I'm cold,' she said.

The ogre carried her, set her down close to the fire, and wrapped her in his best blanket. He hung out her clothes to dry and gave her a bowl of piping hot leek and potato soup. Afterwards, warmed through inside and out, Miranda slept for a while; and the ogre sat and watched her, happier than he had been in his whole life.

By the time she woke, her clothes were dry again, and he rowed her back across the lake, towing her own boat behind them. She talked to him all the while, and that was when she told him of the smiling stranger with the pointed teeth who had just come to lodge in the village.

'No one knows where he came from, but Father says he'll make us all rich. That's what everyone says. He may too, but I don't think so. There's something shifty about him. He smiles too much. Father says he'd make a good husband. I tell you, I'd rather marry a billygoat. Him and his magic Stardust! "What do you want most in the world?" he says. Well, of course, everyone says the same thing, don't they? "We want to be rich."'

The ogre had stopped rowing, leaving the boat drifting towards the quay. 'Stardust. Stardust.' The word rang in his head like a warning bell. '"All you have to do is sprinkle my Stardust into your cornfields," says the smiling stranger,' she went on, '"and your corn will grow faster in a week than in a whole year. Sprinkle Stardust on the lake and before the week's out you'll be catching fish as big as whales." All we have to do is buy his silly Stardust.'

At this the ogre suddenly became very agitated, croaking and cawing as if wracked inside by some terrible pain. She tried to understand him. She tried to calm him. She wasn't to know the terrible story echoing now in his head, how his mother had told him on her deathbed of the smiling stranger who had come to their house just before he was born, and asked her exactly the same question: 'What do you want most in the world?' 'A boy child who will grow big and strong,' she had said. And she paid him all her life savings. 'Sprinkle this magic Stardust on your supper tonight, and you shall have your wish,' the smiling stranger had said, 'and he took the money and rode away on his fine horse. Only weeks later his mother had given birth to a baby boy, bigger and stronger than any man-child ever born, but as ugly as sin and as misshapen as it is possible to be, and with a voice that croaked like a crow.

The ogre reached forward and clasped Miranda's hands, striving all he could to say the words to warn her, but they would not come. 'Don't worry,' she told him. 'I shall come back. I promised to teach you to speak, didn't I? And I shall. I will come tomorrow. Tomorrow I shall teach you my name. I promise. I promise.'

As the boat touched the quay she leaped out and ran away. Suddenly she stopped and turned to him, her hand on her head. 'My straw hat. I think I've lost my straw hat.

But why am I complaining about a silly hat when I have my life? Thank you, thank you for my life.' And the ogre watched her go, until he could see her no more in the gathering dusk.

That evening, as the ogre sat alone and wretched in his lonely cabin, the people of Ballyloch gathered in their hall to hear the smiling stranger with the pointed teeth tell how every one of them could be ten, twenty times as rich, a hundred times as rich inside a week. 'Sprinkle this magic Stardust,' he declared, 'and you will harvest gold.' They all listened in silence, and wondered and believed; but Miranda was not there to hear it.

Nothing ever happened in Ballyloch without the whole world knowing about it. She had been seen coming back from the island with the ogre. As soon as she got home her father had sent her to her room and locked her in. Through the door she had tried to tell him how the ogre had rescued her from drowning, how he was kind and gentle and not at all as everyone said he was. She begged him to let her go back to the island the next day so that she could fulfil her promise and teach him how to speak.

'Never!' thundered her father. 'Promise me you will never go back there, or you will stay in your room till you do, d'you hear me?' But Miranda would promise no such thing.

So she was not there to protest when the villagers bought their sacks of Stardust from the smiling stranger with the pointed teeth. But she *was* watching from her window the next morning as they sprinkled their Stardust all over their cornfields, and out on the dark green lake. From his island, the ogre saw it too, and hung his head in despair. Somehow he had to warn Miranda when she came. Somehow he had to make her understand. All day he sat and watched and waited for her boat, but no boat came anywhere near his island. By nightfall Miranda had still not come.

All night long he sat there, all the next day, all the next week. Still she did not come and she did not come. On the seventh day, cries of delight echoed across the water as the villagers hauled gigantic fish out of the lake, fish so huge they could scarcely drag them into their boats. And the ogre could see clearly enough from the island that the corn in the fields was already twice the height it had been the week before. On the seventh night the ogre sat by the lakeside and listened to the sound of the revelry wafting over the still dark water. He knew it for certain now. There was no hope. She would never come back to him. Those eyes of hers which had promised so much would, like the smiling stranger's magic Stardust, bring nothing but pain.

Distant thunder sounded through the mountains, heralding a storm, but still the ogre did not seek the shelter of his cabin. When the lightning crackled and crashed overhead, he did not move. He wished only that it would strike him dead. When the cold rain lashed down on him and the wind howled across the lake and chilled him to the bone, he sat where he was and prayed he would freeze to death so that he would not have to face the morning.

Morning came though, and he found himself numb all over, but still alive. The storm had passed by. The morning sun broke through the mist and warmed him. Beside him the swans slept, heads tucked under their wings. That was when the ogre first heard the wailing from across the water. Everyone in the village was out in the streets and gazing up at their houses. Every roof in the village had been ripped off and the thatch strewn about the streets. Out in the cornfields there was no corn left standing. Everywhere the people stood dazed and weeping. Many of them were down at the water's edge and looking out over the lake in stunned horror.

Only then did the ogre notice it himself. The lake was no longer dark. It was green, an unnatural green such as he had never seen before. He knelt down by the lakeside and ran his hand through the water. It wasn't the water that was green. It was covered on the surface by a thick layer of slime. Further out, a moorhen bobbed about in it, green all over. She tried to take off, tried to fly, but could not. An otter ran along the shore, not black and glistening as he usually was, but entirely green from head to tail. And fish lay dead in the water, on the shore, everywhere the ogre looked. And his swans, his beloved swans, were gliding through it, dipping their long and lovely necks. He shouted at them to come back, but it was too late. As they washed and preened themselves, every one of them was turning green. Already some of them were choking. He ran to the end of the island to see if the lake was green all around. It was, as far as the eye could see. A solitary duck quacked from in amongst the reeds. She tried to fly, but her feathers were matted and heavy with slime. The ogre knew she was never going to fly again.

As he watched her struggling in vain to clean herself, the ogre noticed Miranda's straw hat floating in amongst the reeds, and around it the only clear, dark water in the entire lake. He waded out and picked it up. One look underneath the dripping hat and his heart surged with sudden hope. All his years of thatching told him it was possible. Miranda's hat proved it. But the lake was dying all around him. Soon not a fish would be left alive, and he knew that unless he could save them in time, all his beloved swans would die too.

He rowed out over the green lake, and as he rowed he saw dead fish floating all around him, bloated, on the water. A drowned cormorant drifted by and a heron aarked in terror from the shore, flapping his great wings in a frantic effort to rid himself of the cloying green cloak that would not let him fly.

For once the people of Ballyloch paid him little attention as the ogre walked amongst them. They were too busy bemoaning their disaster. 'We brought it on

ourselves,' one was saying. 'How were we to know?' said another. 'The stranger promised we'd be rich, and look what ruin he has brought on us instead.' 'We will have no corn to harvest. There will be no fish to catch. We will all starve, all of us.' 'What have we done to deserve this? What have we done?'

The ogre left them and hurried straight to the weaver's house. From her window, Miranda saw him coming and called down to him. 'I tried to come, I tried, but Father forbade me from ever seeing you again. He made me promise I would never go to the island and, when I refused, he shut me in here. I have not been allowed out of my room for a week. And look what has happened in that week. It was the stranger's magic Stardust that did this. I know it was.'

The ogre waved her straw hat in the air, and tried all he could to tell her what he had discovered, but she could make no sense of all his frantic cawing and croaking.

'Just come up and let me out, and then you can tell me. But hurry, hurry, before Father comes back,' she said. The ogre let himself in the front door and climbed the stairs to Miranda's room. Once the door was unlocked, she took him by the hand and they ran out into the weaving shed where they could be alone and unseen. There, with the roof open to the skies, and the thatch strewn all around their feet, the ogre showed her the straw hat and explained the best he could what had to be done in order to save the lake, and the fish, and the swans, and the people of Ballyloch too. When he had finished, she reached up and touched his face tenderly. 'You are no Beastman,' she said. 'You are the *Bestman*, the best man in Ballyloch, the best man in all the world.'

When the people heard the church bell ringing out, they gathered in the village, believing it was the mayor who had called them together. But the mayor was as puzzled as everyone else when out of the church came Miranda, her straw hat in her hand, and looming behind her the huge form of the Beastman of Ballyloch. Her father was spluttering in his fury, but before he could find the words to protest, Miranda began:

'The fish cannot breathe and the birds cannot fly,' she said. 'The lake is poisoned. If it cannot be saved, then we, too, will die with it. Like the otters, like the herons, we cannot live without our fish.'

'Why is the Beastman here?' cried her father, pushing through the crowd. 'I told you to keep away from him.'

'Get him away. We don't want him near the children,' said the mayor. 'Send him back to his island. We don't need him.'

'And who will thatch our roofs now if he does not?' Miranda was angry now, angrier than she had ever been, and they heard it in her voice. No one could answer her. No one dared answer her, not even her father. She spoke only softly, but everyone listened. 'I'm telling you, we need him for more than thatching, too. He has come to save the lake, and he is the only one among us who can.

He can't tell you how, because he can't speak as we do. So, for now, I shall speak for him.'

She held up her straw hat for everyone to see. 'Only a few days ago, this man, this ogre, this mad, bad Beastman, saved me from drowning. He didn't gobble me up, he saved my life. I was wearing this hat when I fell in the lake and I thought I had lost it. He found it this morning, and saw that all around it the water was clear. Look underneath, and you will see how it soaks up the green slime that is choking the life out of our lake. His idea is that we should weave, all of us together, a huge straw carpet and lay it out on the lake. We shall weave it together with flax – Father has enough flax in his weaving sheds to do it. It can be done. It must be done. We have all the straw we need, all the corn broken by the storm, all the thatch lying loose in the streets. Once the carpet is made, we shall tow it out and leave it on the lake to soak up the green slime.'

They stood, mouths agape. No one spoke a word. 'We must have the carpet on the lake by nightfall,' Miranda went on. 'We may be too late already to save all the fish, all the birds, but we may still save most of them if we hurry. We may even save ourselves.'

No one argued, not even her father. Soon every man, woman and child was out gathering the strewn thatch and the battered corn, and spreading it out to be woven into a great straw carpet. All day they toiled, Miranda and the ogre amongst them. For the very first time in his life the ogre felt the warmth of his smile. No one stopped for a moment, not for food, not for drink. They worked till their backs ached, till their hands were raw, until the carpet of straw was woven together at last. When they had finished, it stretched along the lakeside from one end of the village to the other. At dusk, towed by twenty fishing boats, they hauled it out on to the lake and left it floating there. Neither the ogre nor Miranda nor anyone could do any more. Now the straw had to be left to work its magic. How the people of Ballyloch prayed that night that the straw magic would be stronger than the Stardust magic of the smiling stranger. How they prayed that their lake could be saved.

When the ogre rowed home to his island that night, Miranda was with him. Time and again they stopped to scoop half-drowned birds from the slime, so that by the time they reached the island, the bottom of the boat was filled with them, all struggling for life. Once inside his cabin, they cleaned them off as best they could with straw wisps and clean water, and then they set about bringing in all the surviving swans they could find. They, too, had to be cleaned off and washed down, until their feathers were white again and gleaming in the firelight.

All night, as they worked together, Miranda was teaching him. Tired as he was, he was determined to say at least one word by morning. Over and over again he practised 'Miranda', and by morning he could say 'Manda', which, she said, was as good as, if not better than Miranda, anyway. It was a start. There would be many more nights, she said, and many more words.

Both were dreading the coming of the dawn, for the glow of love was over them, and like all lovers they wanted time to stand still. But in the back of their minds, too, was the awful fear that the green slime would still be there in the morning, that the straw carpet might have failed them. They fell asleep by the fire, the swans all around them.

They were woken by the sound of cheering, and ran outside. Every boat in the village, it seemed, was heading towards the island. And the lake was dark once more, and dancing with the early morning sun. The straw magic had worked! There were still some patches of green close to the shore, but they were few and far between. There would be enough clean water now for the fish to breathe, for the birds to wash themselves clean. The people of Ballyloch leaped out on to the grassy bank, hoisted the ogre and Miranda on to their shoulders and carried them off in triumph around the island. Above them flew swans, their wings singing in the air.

Set down at last on their feet again, Miranda kissed away in one minute all the sadness the ogre had stored up inside him all his life. 'This is my man,' she declared joyously. 'This is the *Bestman* in Ballyloch.' And there was not a soul there who disagreed. 'And who,' she asked him, 'who is the best girl in Ballyloch?'

'Manda,' said the Bestman of Ballyloch. 'Manda. Manda.'

By the time they married a few months later, he could say the name of everyone who lived in Ballyloch, and could tell Miranda what every bird he saw was called, and every animal too, come to that. After that he very soon learned to talk well enough to make himself understood. Of course his work was more in demand than ever after the storm damage. Now, wherever he went, he was invited in to eat at their tables and to warm himself at their hearths.

He was mending the roof on the weaving shed when Miranda's father came in, carrying the biggest and most beautiful jacket he had ever made.

'For you,' he said. 'This is to ask your pardon, and to thank you for saving my daughter, for saving all of us.'

The ogre tried it on and it fitted perfectly. 'You do not need to live out on your island any more,' said Miranda's father. 'Come and live with us in the village. You are one of us now.'

'It is kind of you, and this jacket is fit for a prince,' said the ogre. 'But Manda and I, we must stay with our swans.'

It was some time later that their first child was born on the island, a girl child, and she was as healthy and as beautiful as it is possible to be. They were sitting by the fire one evening, the child sleeping in the cradle beside them. The ogre was silent with his own thoughts, thoughts Miranda found she could often guess at just by looking at him. 'She does not know it yet,' he said. 'But when she grows up, she will know I am ugly.'

'You are not ugly!' cried Miranda. 'You are as beautiful as your daughter is beautiful, as beautiful as your swans are beautiful. Do you think I would look twice at a smooth-faced Prince Charming? You're my man, my best man, and don't you forget it. I love you, every bulbous bump of you, every craggy crease of you, you great oaf! Now, off with you and catch my supper.'

'Salmon or trout?'

'Trout tonight,' she said. 'I feel like a nice, fat, brown trout.'

'Well, you don't look like one,' he replied, and he was gone out of the door before she could find anything to throw at him.

A Story that Begins and Ends with Lies

by Sonia Nimr

(PALESTINE)

illustrated by Siân Bailey

Long, long ago in the land of Palestine, there lived a mighty king. His kingdom was vast, his lands were fertile and his riches were beyond count. His people loved him because he was just and kind.

The king had a son who was brave and wise and loved reading. The king wanted his son to get married and have children, but each time the subject of marriage came up, the prince would say that he hadn't found the right girl.

One day, the king said to his son, 'There are many princesses in my kingdom. Why don't you choose one of them to be your wife?'

The prince replied, 'The girl of my dreams doesn't have to be a princess.'

The king said, 'Then choose one from the noble rich families in my kingdom.'

The prince answered, 'She doesn't have to be rich or from a noble family.'

'Find the most beautiful girl in my kingdom,' the king insisted.

'She doesn't have to be beautiful,' the prince said stubbornly.

The king began to lose his patience and asked, 'Who is the girl of your dreams then?'

'She has to be intelligent, smart and know how to tell stories,' the prince said with a smile.

'How are we going to find such a girl?' asked the king doubtfully.

'Easy,' said the prince. 'We will have a party and invite all the girls in the land to attend, and the one who can tell a story that begins and ends with lies will be my future wife.'

Invitations were sent all around the kingdom, and preparations in the palace for the party began.

The big day came, and girls from every part of the kingdom flocked to the palace, each wearing her best clothes and her best looks and each dreaming of being chosen by the prince.

The storytelling began.

A beautiful princess came forward. Her dress was made of the finest silks, her hair was braided with golden thread, and her jewellery was shining in the candlelight. She was as beautiful as a rose and as graceful as a swan. With a voice like the gentle flow of a river, she began her story. 'Once upon a time, there —'

But before she could say another word the prince stopped her with a gesture of his hand and said, 'All stories begin like that; I want a story that begins and ends with lies … '

One by one, the girls began to tell their stories, but all of them failed to impress the prince.

The prince looked bored and was about to leave the party, when suddenly a girl came forward. She was plain, not richly dressed, and her long black hair was arranged in simple braids. With the most spectacular smile the prince had ever seen, she sat in front of him and, without any introduction, she began.

'When my grandparents got married, I was invited to their wedding.'

At this moment, everyone in the great hall fell silent, and the prince smiled for the first time.

'They gave me an egg as a wedding present. It was as big as a watermelon, white as a full moon on a summer night and smooth as the cheek of a baby. I was very happy to have it. I played with it on the way home, throwing it from one hand to the other. But suddenly it fell on the ground and broke into two halves. Out of my egg came a huge rooster. It was as colourful as the meadows in the spring, and as big and strong as a horse. I said to myself, oh well, since it is so big I can ride it instead of a horse.

'On the back of my rooster, I travelled everywhere. Forests, rivers, seas, islands, mountains, valleys, cities and faraway lands. I was enjoying myself so much, that I hadn't noticed that the back of my rooster had become infected.

'I went to the medicine man and asked him for a cure for my rooster. He said, "Take the stone of a date and crush

it at exactly noon, then when the moon is full, spread the oil of the date on his back. By morning, as if by magic, he will be better."

'I did exactly what he said and went to sleep. Next morning I went to check on my rooster and LO AND BEHOLD, a huge palm tree had grown on its back!'

Everybody in the hall was holding their breath.

'On the top of the palm tree there were the biggest, brownest, juiciest dates I have ever seen. I started throwing stones at the top of the tree and the dates began to fall down. I ate ninety-nine dates very slowly, savouring the taste. The hundredth I ate very quickly, as a thought came suddenly into my mind. The stones, which I threw at the top of the tree, didn't come down. So, I decided to climb the tree and find out why not. I was still climbing the tree when the sun went down, so I spent the night sleeping on a branch using pieces of bark as cover. I continued to climb the next day and reached the top before the sun went down again.

'I rubbed my eyes with disbelief. For there, in front of my eyes, stretched the largest and most fertile land.

'Yehhhhhhhhhhh, this is MY land on top of MY tree, which grew on the back of MY rooster, which came out of MY egg.

'I began to think, *What shall I grow on my land?*

'In the end I decided to grow sesame seeds. In the morning I planted the seeds, and in the afternoon the harvest was ready. I began to collect my harvest; I filled thousands of sacks, each with thousands of pounds of sesame seeds.

'When I finished I counted my seeds and found that one was missing. Who took my sesame seed? I looked around and saw an ant holding my seed and running away. I ran after it and got hold of my sesame seed, but the ant was holding on to the other end. So I pulled, and the ant pulled, I pulled, and the ant pulled, until the seed was broken and a SEA of sesame oil came out of it.

'Hurrrrrrrrrah, instead of one, now I had two harvests.

'I began to think about what I should plant on my land next and, after lengthy deliberations, I decided to grow watermelons. I planted the seeds in the morning, and in the afternoon the harvest was ready and my watermelons were ripe.

'I was collecting my watermelons when I noticed a giant BLUE and SQUARE watermelon at the far end of my field. Deciding that it would be the juiciest and tastiest of all, I pulled out my twenty-metre-long sword and made a square cut into it.

'But before I put the piece in my mouth, I noticed a stairwell in my melon. I decided to investigate, so I climbed down the stairs until I reached the bottom. I found a very big market place, people coming and going, selling and buying, shops and goods of all sorts, meat, vegetables, brass pans, pottery jars, leatherwear, books and many other things.

'As I was wandering around I saw an old man sitting on the ground and looking very sad. I came to him and asked what was the matter. The old man pointed to his donkey, which was lying on its back with one leg crossed over the other, one foreleg under its head and the other holding a pipe with smelly smoke coming out of it. The old man said that his donkey was refusing to move and that he had many deliveries to make. I wanted to help, so I told the man to hold its head while I held its tail and together we would make it stand upright.

'One, two, three, pull.

'But the donkey did not move.

'One, two, three, pull.

'But the donkey still would not move.

'One, two, three, pu –.

'The donkey stayed lying on the ground but his tail came off in my hand. When the man saw what had happened, he started to pull his hair and shout and wave his arms. He led a huge number of people who appeared from nowhere, in a demonstration demanding justice.

'I was arrested and taken to jail. On the day of the trial, everybody was suggesting a fitting punishment for me. The judge was still thinking when someone came up with an ingenious idea. "Let's banish the stranger from here." "Yes, YES!" all the others shouted. "Let's put the stranger in the barrel of a cannon and shoot her away."

'The next day, the people gathered to watch as I was squeezed into the barrel of a cannon. I heard them cheer when I was shot into the air. Above the clouds I flew with the birds, and rode on the rainbow. I saw the mountains below me and the people as small as ants. I flew and flew, UNTIL I LANDED AT THE PRINCE'S PARTY.'

The prince smiled. He had finally found the girl he wanted to spend the rest of his life with.

Poetics

by Benjamin Zephaniah
(UNITED KINGDOM)

illustrated by Sara Fanelli

There's a poem on your face
There's a poem in the sky
There's a poem in outta space
There are poems passing by,
There are poems in your dreams
There are poems in your head
Sometimes I cannot get to sleep
'Cause there are poems in me bed.

There are poems in me tea
There are poems on me toast
I have found much poetry
In the place I love the most,
There's a poem right in front of you
Get to know its rhyme,
If you are not sure what to do
Just call it poem time.

There's a poem in me shoes
There's a poem in me shirt

When the poem meets the blues
It can really, really hurt,
Other poems make you grin
When they dribble off your chin
Some poems think they are great
So they like to make you ...
Wait.

I see poems in your teeth
I see poems in me cat
I hear poems underneath
Going rata tat tat tat,
This one has not finished yet
It keeps coming on the beat
It is soggy and it's wet
But it's also very sweet.

There are poems for the ear
There are poems for the page
Some poems are not quite clear
But they get better with age,
There are poems for the hip
There are poems for the hop
Everything is poetic
Poetry will never stop.

There are poems on your fingers
There's a poem on your nose

If you give it time to linger
It will grow and grow and grow,
There's a poem in you beautiful
Can't you see it?
It's right
There.

I think it's so incredible
There are poems
Everywhere.

Whosland

by Benjamin Zephaniah
(UNITED KINGDOM)

illustrated by Satoshi Kitamura

At dawn one morn
After eight weeks of sailing,
The Europeans landed
On the gold, sandy beach.

After praying
They made their way
Inland,
With their flags in their hands
And an empire on their minds.

Soon they came across a small village,
All the people came out to see them,
The villagers thought they had come
with great knowledge
And wisdom from afar
Having never seen Europeans before
This was new and exciting.

'What did you call this land before
we arrived?'
said the captain.

'Ours,'
said the village elder,

'Ours.'

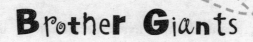

Brother Giants

by Dick King-Smith
(United Kingdom)

illustrated by Jane Ray

Mountain Number One

Once upon a mountain, there lived two remarkable giants named Barrington and Chesterfield.

They were remarkable for several reasons. The first, of course, was their size. Each was twelve feet tall. Each had enormous hands and huge feet and great big noses on their great big faces.

The second was that they were identical twins, something that is rare among giants.

The third was the fact that, although they looked exactly like one another, they were quite different in one respect. Barrington was a meat-eater. Chesterfield was a vegetarian.

This had been the case ever since they were small (for even giants start small). When their giant parents raided the farms and market gardens in the valley below the mountain, they brought back meat – like a nice spring lamb – for little Barrington, and green stuff – like a couple of dozen spring cabbages – for little Chesterfield.

Now, giants do not live especially long lives, and when the twins were only twelve years old and only eight feet tall, both their parents died, which meant Barrington and Chesterfield then had to find their own food.

They found plenty in the rich and fertile valley, and none of the people who lived there dared face the giants. They let them take whatever they wanted, thankful to escape with their lives, for there were other giants in other parts, it was rumoured, that killed people. Some, it was whispered, even ate them.

Time passed and Barrington and Chesterfield grew and grew and grew.

Barrington, of course, ate no vegetables but he did sometimes eat fruit from the orchards.

Chesterfield, of course, never touched meat but he allowed himself milk and eggs and honey.

Twice a week, on Wednesdays and Saturdays, the brothers would come down from their cave in the mountainside, each with a great sack slung over his shoulder, and together they would make the rounds of farms and market gardens, of dairies and hen houses and beehives.

Then back up the mountain they would go with their full sacks. One might contain a fat pig or a sheep, some chickens and a few apples, while in the other there might be carrots and cauliflower and cheeses and eggs and a honeycomb.

Barrington and Chesterfield always did everything together. They walked in step with one another. They woke up or went to sleep at exactly the same time. They even sneezed at the same moment.

Often, as the twin brothers sat side by side, eating a meal in their cave, Barrington would say (as he tore lumps from a leg of lamb), 'What a funny chap you are, Ches, eating all that rabbit food and cheese and muck. I couldn't be doing with that.'

And, as he shoved a whole vegetable marrow into his mouth, Chesterfield would reply, 'It's you that's funny, Barry old boy, chewing your way through all that messy meat. It would make me sick.'

'Well, I'm just glad I'm not a vegetarian,' Barrington would say, and Chesterfield would reply, 'Well, I'm just glad I am, so sucks to you,' and both of them (at exactly the same moment, of course) would burst out laughing.

The sound of their giant laughter would ring round the cave and echo down the mountainside and, in the valley below, mothers would tell their naughty children, 'Behave yourselves, or the giants will get you.'

When Barrington and Chesterfield reached the age of twenty and the height of twelve feet, they stopped growing.

To look at (if anyone had been brave enough to take a good look at them, which no one was) they were impossible to tell apart. Their features were the same, even to parting their hair on the same side, and their huge bodies were identical, except for one thing. Maybe it was to do with all the meat he ate, but Barrington had a very hairy chest. Chesterfield's chest was hairless except for one or two lonely ones.

Each secretly envied the other.

Ches is lucky, thought Barrington, *having a nice smooth chest like that while I've got this jungle growing on mine.*

I wish I had hair on my chest like Barry, thought Chesterfield, *mine's as bare as a desert. If ever we meet a girl, she's sure to like hairy-chested chaps best.*

At the same moment, Barrington was thinking that any girl they met would be certain to prefer smooth-chested giants. For by now, though the twins were still perfectly happy with each other's company, each felt that something was missing in their lives.

Each had girls on his mind.

There were, of course, plenty of girls of marriageable age on the farms and market gardens in the valley below, but neither twin was in the least interested in such midgets, mostly less than five and a half feet tall. No, no, what each was dreaming of was what all healthy normal young giants want – a healthy normal young giantess. There were none on their mountain, but on some other mountain, each said to himself, there must be the giantess of my dreams.

They did not discuss this openly, but one evening after supper, when Barrington had just polished off a baron of beef and Chesterfield was chock full of chickpeas and chives and cheese, they looked at one another and each knew without a doubt what the other was thinking.

With one breath they said, 'It's time I found a wife.'

And the very next morning, off they set.

Mountain Number Two
and Mountain Number Three

Giants, the brothers had been taught by their parents, lived only in the mountains, which they could walk up or down – with their six-foot strides – twice as easily as ordinary folks.

Barrington and Chesterfield wasted no time in the next valley behind their home, but marched across it, side by side and keeping step, and climbed the mountain beyond.

Near its summit, they met a very old, white-haired giant who greeted them gruffly with the words, 'Who are you and what do you want?'

The twins introduced themselves. 'We're looking for wives, sir,' they said politely.

At this, the old giant's manner changed completely. He pulled at his long white beard, and his much-lined face broke into a smile. 'Well, well, boys!' he said. 'I may be able to help you.'

'You have unmarried daughters, sir?' they asked eagerly.

'One daughter. You'd have to toss for her. She's gone to fetch my lunch; she should be back any minute,' said the old giant. 'Sit down, my lads, and tell me all about yourselves. You look very alike.'

'We're twins,' said Chesterfield.

'Indeed? How old are you?'

'Twenty,' said Barrington.

'Twenty!' said the old giant wistfully. 'Lucky lads. Alas, I'm past fifty myself.'

Fifty! thought each twin. *He's got one foot in the grave. Whichever of us gets this girl won't have to support a father-in-law for long.*

Just then, they heard a rattle of stones further down the mountainside and saw a figure striding up the slope towards them.

At first it was only possible to see by its shape that it was a giantess, carrying a dead sheep slung across her shoulders. It was not until the giantess reached them and threw down the sheep that the twins could clearly see her face.

'Now then, boys,' said the old giant, 'this is my daughter.'

The boys stared speechlessly at the young giantess. They noted her thick black eyebrows, the dark shadow of a moustache on her upper lip, her brown uneven teeth bared in a smile of welcome, and the many spots upon her chin.

'Pretty as a picture, isn't she?' said the old giant.

'Which one of you is going to marry her?'

'I won't stand in your way, Ches,' said Barrington hurriedly.

'No, no,' said Chesterfield hastily. 'I won't steal your thunder, Barry.'

The young giantess leered at them. 'I wouldn't mind marrying both of them, Daddy,' she said.

Chesterfield cast a despairing glance at Barrington, and his brother returned it.

'We'll have to go away,' they said, 'and talk it over. We'll let you know when we've decided,' and then with giant strides they plunged away down the mountainside.

Behind them they heard the voice of the giantess crying, 'Don't be long! I'll be waiting!'

'She'll be waiting all right,' said Chesterfield as they hurried away across the next valley.

'Forever, I should think,' said Barrington.

For a while they marched on, side by side and keeping step, and then Barrington said, 'I've been thinking, Ches.'

'So have I, Barry,' said Chesterfield, 'and I've had an idea.'

'Me too,' said Barrington. 'If we do meet a decent-looking girl, we shall only be competing against one another.'

'Exactly. But if we split up for a while, each of us might find what he's looking for on his own.'

'Exactly.'

So when they reached the next mountain, each went his separate way, Barrington up one side and Chesterfield up the other.

It was not long before Barrington came upon a young giantess sitting upon a rock, eating raw runner beans. He looked closely as he approached. She wasn't bad looking, quite a handsome piece in fact. *There's no time to waste*, he thought. So he said to her, 'Hullo and are you married and if not will you marry me?'

'You're a fast worker,' she said. 'The answers are – no, I'm not, and it depends.'

'Depends on what?'

'Whether you eat meat.'

'Of course I do,' said Barrington.

'In that case,' said the giantess, 'I wouldn't marry you if you were the last giant on earth. I'm a vegetarian.'

Wow! thought Barrington. *Just right for my brother.* And he hurried away, shouting, 'Ches! Ches! Where are you?'

Chesterfield was round the other side of the mountain, and he too had come across quite an attractive young giantess who was sitting upon a rock, gnawing a beef bone.

'Hullo,' he said. 'I'm looking for a single girl with a view to marriage. Any chance you're free?'

'You don't mess about, do you?' she replied. 'Yes, I'm free. Have a bit of my bone.'

'No thanks,' said Chesterfield. 'I'm a vegetarian.'

'Well, get lost then,' said the giantess. 'The giant I marry has got to be a meat-eater like me.'

Wow! thought Chesterfield. *Just right for my brother.* And he hurried away, shouting, 'Barry! Barry! Where are you?'

When the brothers had met and told one another what had happened, each set off round the mountain to meet the giantess the other had found. It was a hot day, and they stripped off their shirts and tied the arms around their waists.

Each now knew that both the giantesses were single, so when Barrington found the beef-eater, he pitched straight in. 'Will you marry me?' he said. 'I'm a meat-eater like you.'

'No chance,' said the giantess.

She pointed her beef bone at Barrington and said, 'If there's one thing I can't stand, it's giants with hairy chests.'

When Chesterfield came upon the bean-eating giantess, he too wasted no words. 'I'm a vegetarian like you,' he said. 'Will you marry me?'

'Not a hope,' said the giantess.

She pointed a runner bean at him and said, 'One thing that really turns me off is a giant with a smooth chest.'

When the brothers met once again, Barrington said, 'It looks as though I've got to give up eating meat. Which I shan't.'

'Or,' said Chesterfield, 'I've got to grow a lot of hair on my chest. Which I can't.'

'I didn't really fancy her anyway,' they both said at the same moment.

'Talk about fussy,' said Barrington. 'Why can't they be easygoing like us?'

'Exactly,' said Chesterfield. 'Why can't a giantess be more like a giant?' And side by side and keeping step, they marched away towards the next mountain.

Mountain Number Four

'Maybe this mountain will be lucky, Ches,' said Barrington as they reached its foot.

'Hope so, Barry,' replied Chesterfield, and each crossed two of his eight-inch fingers. Then they went their separate ways up the steep slopes.

On the eastern side of the mountain Chesterfield met a family of giants. They made him very welcome, offering him a whole suckling pig (which of course he refused, pretending that he had just eaten). There was a mother giant and a father giant and three giant children, all boys.

'Fine sons you have,' said Chesterfield. 'No daughters?'

'No,' said the mother.

'You married?' asked the father.

'No.'

Father and mother looked at each other and smiled.

'Try the other side of the mountain,' they said.

On the western side Barrington was in a daze of happiness. Halfway up, he had paused to rest awhile and was admiring the view below when he heard steps behind him. He turned to see a giantess. And what a giantess!

The first one they'd met had been so ugly that, by

contrast, the beef-eater and the bean-eater had seemed handsome, but this girl was beautiful!

She was almost as tall as him – perhaps eleven and a half feet, and her hair was corn-coloured and her eyes sea-blue and her teeth pearly white. Barrington stared at her, dumbstruck.

'Hullo,' she said in a voice like warm treacle. 'Who are you?'

Barrington smiled. 'My name's Barrington,' he said, 'but you can call me Barry if you like.'

'My name,' said the beautiful giantess, 'is Georgina, but you can call me Georgie. Can I do anything for you?'

Oh yes, thought Barrington, *you can be my wife! This is it! This is the real thing! This is love at first sight!*

'Tell me you're not married,' he said.

'I'm not,' said Georgina.

'Tell me you're not a vegetarian.'

'I like all sorts of food.'

Blushing furiously, Barrington undid the buttons of his shirt. 'Tell me,' he said, 'that you don't mind hairy chests.'

Georgina burst out laughing. It was a jolly bubbly laugh, an infectious laugh, and Barrington found himself laughing with her.

'No,' she said. 'I don't mind.'

They stared at one another, and then Barrington reached out and took her huge hand in his even huger one.

'Georgie,' he said.

'Yes, Barry?'

'I am looking for a wife.'

'Look no further,' she said.

'Oh, Georgie!' said Barrington. 'You have made me the happiest giant in the world.'

Just then they heard a voice calling, 'Barry! Barry! Where are you?'

'Who's that?' asked Georgina.

'My twin brother, Ches,' said Barrington. 'It's short for Chesterfield.'

'Your twin brother?' said Georgina.

'Yes.'

'Identical?'

'Yes,' said Barrington. 'He's looking for a wife too,' and then, as Chesterfield came into sight, 'but it doesn't look as though he's had any luck.'

'Ches, old boy,' he said when his brother reached them, 'allow me to introduce Georgina, Georgie for short.'

Chesterfield stared at her, speechless. *This is it*, he thought. *This is the real thing! This is love at first sight!*

'I hope you'll be very happy, Ches,' said Barrington (*We shall*, thought Chesterfield), 'to know that Georgie and I are engaged to be married. It was love at first sight.'

Somehow, Chesterfield managed a smile. Somehow, he stammered out words of congratulation. He stood and watched as the happy couple descended the slopes and set off, hand in hand, across the valley, on their way home. Then he sat down and put his giant head in his giant hands.

For a long time he sat there, the picture of misery. *If only I had gone round the western side and Barry round the eastern,* he thought. *As it is, he is to marry the giantess of my dreams. I shall never meet another like her. And what's more, I shall never see my twin brother again — I couldn't bear to go home and play gooseberry. Two's company, three's none.*

He heaved a giant sigh.

'You don't sound very happy,' said a voice like warm treacle.

Chesterfield raised his head to see Georgina standing before him, showing her pearly-white teeth in a smile, her sea-blue eyes twinkling, her corn-coloured hair blowing in the mountain breeze.

She's come back! he thought. *She's decided against poor old Barry; she's chosen me instead!*

'Oh,' he said. 'You're not going to marry Barry.'

The giantess looked puzzled.

'Marry Barry?' she said. 'Certainly not.'

Chesterfield swallowed. 'I have to tell you that I'm a vegetarian,' he said.

'Doesn't worry me.'

'And also that I haven't got any hairs on my chest, except for one or two lonely ones.'

'I don't much like hairy chests.'

Chesterfield took a deep breath. 'In that case,' he said, 'will you marry *me*?'

'I quite like that idea,' said the beautiful giantess. 'Though I haven't a clue who you are.'

'But I'm Chesterfield. Ches for short. Don't you remember me, Georgie?'

'No,' said the giantess, 'because I'm not Georgie. I'm Alexandra, though you can call me Alex.'

'I don't understand,' said Chesterfield. 'How can you be so *exactly* like Georgie?'

'Because,' said Alexandra, 'she and I are identical twins.'

Magic

by Meshack Asare
(GHANA)

illustrated by Alex Ayliffe

The shadows disappeared in the twilight as the sun slipped behind the low hills in the west. It was Alide's favourite time, the moments just before everything sank into total darkness and kerosene lamps cast dancing shapes on walls and ceilings. Everything became the same then. Houses looked alike and people turned into faceless, talking silhouettes. The half-light wrapped all up into one.

But it was not only the light. By now, dogs only barked when they were themselves bitten. Conversations took on low, even tones. And, as wooden mortars pounded corn and yam for the evening meals, they sent their cheers booming up to the sky, toom-tam-toom-tam-toom. The air was spiced with stews, soups and sauces. That was the time.

Father was at the veranda, straining his eyes over a newspaper. Whether it was from tiredness or from trying to read news he'd heard many times over, it was one yawn after another. Little Keli was playing by himself nearby, croaking like a frog. Mother was in the kitchen with Muko.

It was Alide's job to clean the three lanterns of the house

and she was busy at it. First she cleaned the new lantern, the big shiny one with a net inside that made white light like the full moon, the *Aladdin*.

'Alide,' Father had said when he brought this lamp from town, 'I've brought you an *Aladdin* lamp. It will sit on the cupboard in the front room and give you all the light you need. Now you can read as much as you like, but you must take care of it.'

'Aladdin's lamp?' she asked curiously. 'The magic lamp?'

'Magic?' Father wondered for a moment. 'Ah, I see what you mean,' he said, his face brightening up. 'In fact this lamp too has magic. But you'll have to find out for yourself.'

Everyone came to look as Father unpacked and assembled it. Indeed it was like magic when he filled it with kerosene, pumped it up and lit it with a match. With a pop, a tongue of flame jumped up, fluttered a bit, and turned into a solid cone of white light. It was so bright, that for a while it dazzled the eyes. But soon everyone got used to it. That was three weeks ago.

On this evening, like many evenings before, Alide cleaned the *Aladdin*. The glass shade was as clear as rainwater and she topped up the kerosene as Father had shown her to do. She cleaned the second lamp, an ordinary storm lantern, and placed it next to the *Aladdin*. Last was the one that left rings of kerosene wherever it stood, though it had been soldered many times by the tinker at the market place.

She picked it up by the wire arm; she always picked it up that way. But this evening, for whatever reason, it felt like lead. So she decided to lift it up with more force. The old lamp left the floor, hung in the air for a moment and swung away from her. Before she knew it, it started to swing back towards her with more weight than before. She was unable to stop it. The bottom of the old lamp smashed heavily into the middle of the *Aladdin* – c–r–a–c–k! The clean glass shade of the gleaming new lamp tinkled like beads on the cement floor.

Alide's heart missed several beats and, for a moment, she saw nothing. When the darkness cleared, there was shattered glass all around her and Father was holding the twisted, empty frame of the *Aladdin* in his hands, with Keli staring curiously at it.

'What is it?' Mother enquired from the kitchen. Alide was tongue-tied and couldn't answer. It was Father who replied. 'It's the *Aladdin* lamp. It's shattered. We can't use it any more. It has to be thrown away.'

'What happened?' Mother asked again.

'Don't know, but it was a terrible noise. Alide, are you all right?'

Still in a daze, she did not answer. She was trembling when Father put down the mangled lamp and stretched an arm to her.

'That was strange,' he said to her, 'but you are not hurt and that is good. Maybe we made the old lantern jealous of the *Aladdin*. Jealousy is everywhere you know, even among lamps. Now you will have to read by the old light again.'

Without the white light from the *Aladdin* it seemed like being in the shade. It was not the twilight that she loved and it was not the night with the full moon. It felt strange. That evening, Alide ate her supper, but only because she had to. She found none of the tastes and smells that she always enjoyed from eating. She'd never felt so sorry for herself before.

Mother said to her, 'Alide, don't feel so sorry for yourself. It was an accident. You could even have been hurt, but you are safe. Papa will get us a new one soon. Now cheer up.' But nothing could cheer her up. She liked the *Aladdin* a lot and she had smashed it.

Later, in the front room, Muko was at his usual place at the table, doing his homework. Mother and Father were on the veranda and Keli was in bed. Alide sat on the floor as she always did, in front of the cupboard. She brought out her book, leaned against the wall and opened it. The light came from the old lantern on the cupboard.

Alide looked up for a moment and began to think of Father's strange words: 'Maybe we made the old lantern jealous of the *Aladdin*. Jealousy is everywhere.'

All the same, I broke it and I cannot forgive myself, she thought.

'You can't forgive yourself for what?' a voice asked from somewhere.

'Look, whoever you are, I've wrecked the *Aladdin* lamp and I feel miserable.'

'You feel miserable for wrecking a lamp?'

'Not just a lamp,' said Alide, 'it is the *Aladdin*.'

'My dear child,' the voice said again. 'If you knew the troubles other people have, then you'd see how tiny yours are and how lucky you are.'

'This is the worst thing that happened to me. I could die,' said Alide.

'No. No. No,' said the voice. 'I will show you something. Just open your book.'

At other times she would have liked to know whose voice it was. But now, overcome with sadness about the broken lamp, she quietly did as she was told. Alide opened the book. But suddenly, she was no longer looking at a book but into a window. Through the window she saw a donkey. But it was not an ordinary donkey. The pelt of this donkey was all gold. Alide was surprised and even as she wondered, the voice asked her, 'What do you see in the window?'

'A donkey,' she answered. 'A golden donkey.'

'A-ha,' said the voice knowingly. 'You think that is a donkey, but he's not. In fact, he is a prince. Now he's been sold and bought so many times over, he should be dead. But there he is.'

'So — so how did he become a donkey?' Alide stammered.

'He will tell you, if you ask him,' answered the voice. 'You only broke a lamp and wish you were dead. Now ask him how he turned from a prince into a donkey,' the voice urged her.

Before she opened her lips to speak, the golden donkey drew closer to the window and began, 'I owe the way I am now to my own folly. I fell in love with a maiden and wanted to visit her. But I wanted to fly to her. That would have impressed her immensely.'

'Yes,' Alide agreed. 'But – but that should not ...'

'There was only one way to fly,' said the donkey. 'We had no flying machines. We only had magic. But that was no problem. I knew another maiden, the apprentice of the most powerful magician in the land. We were very good friends so I asked her for help. She was quiet for some time when I asked her. But after the long silence, she agreed to help me. She told me the times her mistress was away and we made a date. I was with her at the appointed hour and you can imagine how excited I was!'

The donkey paused and remained silent for a while. Tears rolled down his face to the ground. Looking more closely, Alide noticed that the teardrops had a sheen. There were small piles of them by his feet, each droplet a nugget that shimmered like the moonlight.

'So even his teardrops are gold!' Alide remarked.

'Yes,' said the voice, 'but he's still very distressed after all these years. He'll continue in a moment, just bear with him.'

That gave Alide an idea. Who was the voice talking to her?

'You are wondering who I am,' the voice said.

'Yes. How do you know?' asked Alide.

'I know because I know nearly everything under the sun and the moon and stars. I know things in the sky above, deep in the ocean, even things beneath. I know things from the past and everything that we know now. Maybe even the future is here within me now.'

'Then you must be extremely clever. But you still haven't said who you are.'

'You should be able to guess who I am,' said the voice. 'We are very good friends, you and I. I am the Spirit of the Book. In any case, he is ready now. He'll tell you how it happened.'

And the donkey resumed. 'The great magician was away; it was deepest night. I was alone with my friend the maiden, the magician's apprentice. We were in the magician's *sanctum,* surrounded from floor to ceiling by phials, jars and vessels of every description and colour.

'By then I could not bear the excitement. I imagined myself soaring into the sky, moonbeams glinting off my back, a great silver bird. I imagined myself hovering and circling over the dwelling of my beloved. I imagined myself landing before her door with a huge flutter of wings, the hero. I shivered. I trembled with my own excitement.'

There was another pause, but this time there were no tears in his eyes. He only swung his short, golden tail from side to side and continued. 'My friend the maiden reached for a small coffer of ebony and ivory. She set it down on a table before me and lifted the top open. There were nine phials in it, I can't tell what colours they were.

'With a gleam in her eyes, she lifted one phial and held it to me. "Here you are," she said confidently. "Drink it and you will know the wonders of flight." I took the tiny bottle in my hand and tipped its content into my mouth. I could feel it coursing down my throat. I felt its warmth inside my stomach, and soon it rose to the surface of my skin.

'I remember her watching me, and somehow the gleam in her eyes had disappeared. That should have made me think. After all she too was a maiden, pretty as any princess one could lay eyes on. I knew from all the times she entertained me that she must have cared for me a great deal.

'But the heart in my chest was beating for someone else and maybe hers was choking with jealousy. For suddenly, her face was like a mask carved out of ice. Then, with any hint of friendliness gone, she extended a hand to my ear and led me to the mirror. "*Now fly*," she said. And only then a smile came to her face. "Fly wherever you want." I looked into the mirror but I did not see myself, the tall, gallant, handsome prince. I saw what you see before you now, a golden donkey. Beside me was the maiden with a smile that said everything that I feared: jealousy, revenge, foolishness. But it was late. Too late.'

Alide's heart nearly stopped. But the voice came back, 'Imagine his anxiety,' it said. 'I'm sure you have questions on the tip of your tongue. But we must leave him. Come. Turn another page in your book. I'll show you something else.'

Alide turned the page and another window opened before her. This time it was a vista beginning from the window and stretching far into the distance.

There were mountains, hills, valleys, lakes, rivers, fields, forests, skies. There were suns, moons, stars, animals, roads, curves, slopes, toads, trees. Before her eyes, a young woman appeared. She looked very pretty but also angry. It was as if she was looking for someone. She turned her head from left to right and peered into the distance ahead of her. She never said a word. Then she did something. She took one step to the side and the road was before her like a ribbon with many folds and curves.

With no effort whatsoever, she took her end of the road in both hands and pulled. She pulled and pulled and the curves began to straighten out. She pulled for the last time and the road became as straight as a yardstick. She gave a sigh, for not too far ahead now, was a young man running desperately away from her.

'I've got you,' the woman said gleefully as she swiped the entire vista with her hand.

Alide's breath rushed out with a hiss. The man disappeared just as the woman's fingers and thumb met in a clasp. But the hand only clawed at thin air. That instant, a fine bird – a kite – hovered over the clasped hand and, with a flutter of wings, flew into the sky. The angry look on the woman's face said that it was not over yet. Indeed, she gave a deafening shout that made Alide stir. 'I'll get you in the end,' she yelled. 'Your magic can't save you from me forever. I'll get you. It's not finished yet. Never!'

'Turn another page in your book, but oh, find your own words for this woman and the man who escapes from her,' the voice said again.

By now Alide had forgotten all about the broken *Aladdin* lamp. And as she knew the voice, she quickly turned a page, and another window opened before her. Guess what is in the window. Take your book and be prepared for a surprise. Open it.

Seriously Weird

by Jean Ure
(UNITED KINGDOM)

illustrated by Sue Heap

It is a fact that there are two sorts of houses: those with books, and those without. Some houses you go into where you can hardly move for books. There are books from floor to ceiling. Books on shelves, books on tables; books in the bedroom, books in the bathroom; books on bookshelves, books in boxes. Books all over the place!

And then there are other houses where you look in vain: can't find a book anywhere. This was the sort of house that Arran lived in. Not a book to be seen! Until you got to Arran's bedroom, and there they all were, neatly stacked in rows. Dozens upon dozens of them, in strict alphabetical order. Across the mantelshelf they marched, across the window sill, across the desk, across a shelf above the bed. Arran was into books in a big way. For Christmas and for birthdays he always gave his mum and dad a list of new titles that he wanted, and asked his gran and his aunties and uncles for book tokens. Last Christmas he'd been given a Harry Potter, *Harry Potter and the Goblet of Fire*. By Boxing Day he'd finished it, all

700 pages. His mum accused him of skipping.

'You can't possibly have read the whole book!'

But he had.

'Shocking waste of money,' grumbled his dad. 'Only lasted him five minutes!'

Arran's dad really resented spending money on books. He wouldn't have minded spending twice, or even three times as much on a computer game because, as he said, you could play a computer game over and over.

'Once you've read a book, that's it! Finished.'

Arran had tried explaining that you could *re-read* a book – 'Lots of times!' – but his dad didn't believe him. His dad didn't even read books once, let alone lots of times. He read the newspapers, and that was that. He didn't see the point of books. You had television, you had videos, you had computers. What would you want a book for?

'Well, because they're different,' said Arran.

'You mean, they're *boring*,' said his sister.

Sherrill didn't read books either, not if she could help it. Nor did Arran's mum, though she was a bit more sympathetic.

'Let him be,' she said. 'It's a harmless enough occupation. At least it keeps him out of trouble.'

'There is that to be said,' agreed Dad, but he didn't sound too enthusiastic. Arran sometimes thought that Dad would prefer him to be almost anything – a football hooligan, a tearaway, a troublemaker – rather than a bookworm. Whenever he settled down to read, Dad always seemed to find something else for him to do.

'Come on, chum! You're wanted downstairs.'

Come and be sociable – come and clean the car – come and watch football, come and watch sport.

'*Get your nose out of that book!*'

But Arran only felt comfortable when his nose was in a book.

'Seriously weird,' said Sherrill.

He didn't see that it was any more weird than painting your fingernails all different colours, or putting red and green stripes in your hair, which was what his sister had recently taken to doing. Dad didn't go on at her.

'This is *fashion*,' said Sherrill, in withering tones.

'Yeah? Well, this is learning,' said Arran.

'Learning? Call that *learning*? Reading books about wizards? Fat lot of good that'll do you!'

'I don't only read books about wizards,' said Arran.

'No? So what else d'you read?'

'I read everything!'

It was true: Arran read whatever he could lay his hands on. If he couldn't find a book, he'd read the backs of cornflake packets, or even the tops of matchboxes. His greatest fear was the thought of being trapped somewhere – on a tube train, for instance – without having anything to read. Once a month they all drove round the M25 to visit Uncle Trevor and Auntie Fay in Brentwood. Mum wouldn't let him take a book; she said it was rude to go to someone else's house and sit and read.

'Extremely bad manners!'

It made him very nervous, because what if there was a hold-up on the M25? What if the car broke down? They could be stuck there for hours! He put this to Mum.

'What'd we do?'

'We'd talk,' said Mum. 'You remember talk? When your lips move?'

Mum thought she was being funny; she didn't know how nerve-racking Arran found it, going somewhere without a book. Occasionally he'd tried stuffing a paperback in his pocket, but Mum always saw it and made him take it out again.

'We'll have no reading on this trip!'

One day his worst nightmare almost came true. The car didn't break down, and they didn't get caught in any traffic jams, but there was football on the television and *they all wanted to watch it*. Not just Dad and Uncle Trevor, but Mum and Sherrill and Auntie Fay. All of them! Except Arran. Arran didn't go for football. He just didn't; it was one of those things. Like they didn't go for reading, he didn't go for football. There wasn't any law said he had to. He didn't see what was so peculiar, not wanting to watch football.

'Just suffer it for once,' said Dad. 'Give it a go! You might surprise yourself.'

He suffered it for forty minutes before boredom set in

and he began to get twitchy. He needed something to read! But there wasn't anything. This was another house without books. Arran's gaze roved desperately round the room. Not a single book anywhere to be seen! Except – his hand crept out. There, on top of the telephone directories . . . what was that? A book!

Slowly, slowly, he drew it towards him. A great shout went up and he started, guiltily. But it wasn't anything to do with him. Someone had scored a goal! Dad and Uncle Trevor did a high five. Sherrill shrieked, '*Yessss!*' Mum cheered. Auntie Fay cried, '*Eng-land!*' and thumped on the arm of her chair. Arran snatched greedily at his book. What was it, what was it?

A car manual. His heart sank. He had no interest in cars. As far as he was concerned, they were just things that took you from place to place. He didn't even like them very much. They polluted the atmosphere and killed wildlife and on long journeys they always made him sick. But even a car manual was better than nothing. Frowning, he settled down to read it.

'I hope that was interesting,' hissed Mum, when the football came to an end and she discovered what he had been doing.

'It was, quite,' said Arran.

'You are *so-o-o* freaky,' said Sherrill.

One morning, two weeks later, Dad couldn't start the car. They were all going off to Gran's, this time. They sat there while Dad fretted and fumed and revved up the engine.

'What's the matter with it?' said Mum.

'It *won't start*,' said Dad, through gritted teeth. He always grew very angry when anything went wrong with the car.

'Why won't it start?' said Sherrill.

'How am I expected to know?' roared Dad. 'Am I a car mechanic?'

'No, dear,' said Mum. 'Of course you're not. Just be quiet, Sherrill! Your dad's trying to concentrate.'

There was a pause. Dad went on revving.

'We'll be late,' said Sherrill.

In the driving mirror, Arran could see Dad's face turning purple. Sherrill really had *no* tact.

'Sounds to me,' said Arran, 'like it's something to do with the distributor ... distributor cap, most probably.'

Dad froze. 'I beg your pardon?'

'Distributor cap,' said Arran.

Sherrill giggled. Dad brought his fist down on top of the steering wheel.

'Well, thank *you*, Mr Motor Vehicle Expert! And what do you know about it?'

'I'm just telling you what I think,' said Arran. 'Distributor cap ... that's my bet.'

In the end, Dad had to call out the breakdown service. They got to Gran's almost two hours late.

'So what exactly was the problem?' said Gran.

Dad's face turning PURPLE!

'The ... ah −' Dad cleared his throat. 'The distributor cap.'

'Arran said that it was,' said Mum.

'My! What a clever boy.' Gran beamed at him. 'How on earth did you know a thing like that?'

'Oh, just something I read,' said Arran.

The New Madam

by Lynne Reid Banks
(UNITED KINGDOM)
illustrated by Peter Bailey

Amayi came bursting into our house that time, looking completely different from how she usually did.

Usually when she got home for her once-a-month visit she was so tired from the long bus ride and the long walk that, after she'd hugged us all, she just wanted to sit down and rest. Then I'd brew her some tea and give her a dish of mealie meal with whatever we had to give it a nice taste. Later she'd open her bundle and then we'd maybe have a treat that she'd brought from her madam's house where she worked in Harare. Then, only then, she'd talk, and tell us all the news.

But this day she was panting with her news as well as from tiredness.

'Mrs Bailey's left!' she cried out.

We were dumb with shock. How could her madam leave? What would happen to Amayi – to us, without a madam to pay her for her housework?

'How do you mean, left?' we all asked at once.

Amayi sank on to one of the mattresses. 'She's gone,

that's all. She sold the house and went back to England. She said — she said she couldn't live in a black-run Zimbabwe any more, she said it wasn't safe for a white woman alone.'

We waited silently, the five of us — me, my three brothers, Welly, Joseph and Robert, and our baby sister Jeena. The baby was on Amayi's knee already. Amayi only had to sit down near to the ground and Jeena crawled into her lap. I tried to be her mother in between Amayi's visits, but she loved Amayi best. The boys were crowded in front of her and I was standing facing her, looking down on the top of her beautiful head with its thick crinkly hair. Amayi was the most beautiful person in our world.

'Here's what happened. She came out to the hut three days ago. She said, "Gertie, I'm going back to England. The house is sold and you'll have a new madam." I started to cry. It's not that I like her so much. But I didn't know what would happen. I said, "What if she doesn't want me?" She said, "Don't be silly, of course she'll want you, you go with the house. Now come and help me to pack my things." And that's all I've been doing for three days is help her pack up. Yesterday a big van came and took away nearly all the furniture. And this morning a taxi came and took her to the airport and she's gone.'

There was a long silence. I turned around to make some tea. After a while Joseph said, in a little voice not like him, 'Can you stay with us then?' Amayi said, 'No. If

I'm not there when the new madam comes, she'll get another person to cook and clean for her, and then what'll we do for money?'

My amayi tells people she's a widow. But truly my daddy ran off and left us just before Jeena was born. I remember him real good, he was big and boomy and fun to play with, but young girls thought that too and he ran off with one of them to Bulawayo. That's why I had to leave school, to look after the others so Amayi could get housework in the city. That's why we only saw her once a month for a weekend. That's why we hardly had any spending money and even for food I sometimes had to borrow.

Now this. And I knew she was right about going back, because what she earned was all we had to live on.

So we got on with the visit and didn't say much more about the new madam. Amayi asked all the usual questions about how the boys were getting on at school. Joseph and Robert were all right, but Welly just said he was sick of it and wanted to leave.

'Why are you sick of it? You're a smart boy, you should like to learn,' Amayi scolded.

'I've learnt all I need to. I hate school.'

I jumped in and told Amayi how much help Welly was, how he'd mended the pipe that brought the water and how he'd taken the old bike to pieces and put it back together with a better brake. Amayi just grunted. This wasn't the kind of smart she wanted for Welly. I was scared Amayi's precious visit would be spoilt and I did everything I could to make her cheerful.

But I saw Amayi getting more and more nervous as it came near time for her to go back.

'I'm scared, Crystal,' she said.

'Of the new madam?'

'Yes, but not only. I'm scared of before she comes. I'm scared to be alone on the place with no one in the Big House.'

In Harare, Amayi lived in a house called the hut, down at the end of the garden of the Big House. I'd never seen it but she described it. It didn't have a floor, just earth, or a proper ceiling, just roof beams, and no electricity. She had some furniture that Mrs Bailey didn't want. Her clothes were mostly Mrs Bailey's cast-offs, too, and her food was what Mrs Bailey gave her. Everything came from Mrs Bailey. Or more often didn't come, because Mrs Bailey didn't understand that Amayi wouldn't buy anything for herself because she needed all her wages for us. I know Amayi went hungry sometimes, even though she never said so (like I never told her that sometimes we did, too).

There were men around the place, to do the grounds. I understood why Amayi didn't want to go back without Mrs Bailey there.

But she had to.

Welly and I walked her all the way to the bus on the Sunday evening. Amayi kissed us and said, as she always did, 'See you in a month!'

But none of us knew what that month would bring.

We didn't expect to hear from Amayi before the month was up. So it was a shock when Mr Mfosa from the Township office came to our door three weeks later and said to come to the phone.

It was Amayi. She'd had to sit on the line for ten minutes while Mr Mfosa fetched me.

'Crystal, is that you?' She sounded different, excited. And she was yelling into the phone.

'Yes, Amayi, don't shout, I hear you!'

'You have to bring Welly to Harare!' She was still shouting.

'Me? Why?'

'Because he's only eleven and he can't come alone!'

I held the phone away from my ear.

'But why do you want him?'

'The new madam's come and *she* wants him!'

'Amayi, please talk quieter! What does she want him for?'

'She –' There was a silence. Then she went on, almost in a whisper. 'She wants to send him to school.'

'He goes to school here.'

'A ... a private school. A good school.'

I didn't believe what I was hearing. A white madam, wanting to send a black kid to a private school?

'Amayi ... Are you sure? Maybe you've got it wrong.'

'I have not! Here, if you don't believe me – ask her.'
There was a noise of talking on the other end and then
I heard a woman's voice.

'Hallo, Crystal? My name is Pauline. I'm the person
who bought Mrs Bailey's property. I want you to come
to Harare and bring your eldest brother. Can the others
manage without you for a couple of days? Is there
anyone you could leave them with?'

I thought quickly. Our next-door neighbour might
take them in if I paid her something for their food.

'I think so. But I don't know how to come.'

'Your mama will tell you. You just have to sit on the
bus till you get to Harare. Then you can take a taxi. I'll
pay when you get here.'

I was stood there not able to talk. A bus trip to Harare,
just me and Welly! Meeting the new madam, seeing where
Amayi lived, seeing the city! I'd only seen the city twice, a
tiny bit of it, never the big houses we'd heard about.

'Well, Crystal? What do you say, will you come on
Saturday?'

'Yes,' I said, croaking like a frog. 'We'll come.'

Amayi said to pack up all Welly's things, but I couldn't. It
would mean he was going for good and I couldn't
imagine life in our house without him. Anyway, I didn't
have anything except plastic bags to put stuff in.

Welly came along because I made him, but he didn't
want to, and when we were on the bus he was very quiet.

He just sat there looking out of the window.

'Aren't you a bit excited?' I asked at last, to break the silence.

'No.'

'You're too smart for the Township school. It'd be good for you to go to a good school.'

'I'm not going to no good school. It's all a mistake. They don't take black kids in private schools.'

'Pauline knows better than you.'

He turned to me. 'Pauline's a first name. You shouldn't call her that.'

It bothered me, too. Whoever heard of calling a white madam by her first name?

The depot was scary, more people than I'd ever seen all together, and noise and pushing and heat and smells. The taxi drivers weren't about to take a couple of scruffily dressed black kids to a white suburb when they couldn't show any money – I'd spent the last I had on the bus fare. Some of them laughed at us. Finally I was crying, and one of the drivers felt sorry for me.

'You got a phone number?'

I gave him the piece of paper I'd written it all down on. He left his car and went off and telephoned. When he came back he was grinning.

'Why didn't you tell me she pay the other end?' I had, of course. Then he added, 'That sounds like a real nice lady.'

We got in the taxi and he drove and drove. The city was so big! Welly was glued to the window, he was leaning halfway out like he was trying to be part of it. The streets, so crowded and noisy and exciting — little shops and stalls and thousands of people, then a district with huge tall buildings and smart cars — and later, here they were! Beautiful quiet streets with big trees covered with blue blossom shading them and lots of high walls and green grass. And big iron gates. Sometimes we could see dogs behind them.

Welly saw them too. 'I wonder what happened to Mrs Bailey's dog,' he said. Amayi'd told us about Sharky, a big fierce wolf-dog. I hoped she'd taken him back to England with her, but Welly said, 'I hope he's still there!'

At last the taxi drew up facing a big gate. He honked his horn, and the gates slowly swung open all by themselves. Wally was amazed but I knew it was electricity. And there was Sharky! He came racing towards us, barking like mad. He looked like the kind of dog that would bite your hand off. I shrank up to Welly and he rolled up the window.

But then Amayi came running. And behind her was a white woman who shouted, 'Be quiet, Sharky! Sit!' And would you believe it? He did! Amayi flung the door open and pulled us out and hugged and hugged us. She was crying but they were happy tears, I could see. All they did was make her smile wet.

'Come and meet Madam!' she said.

The new madam was quite young, well, not young, but she had dark hair and green eyes and she was wearing jeans and a T-shirt and a cigarette in the middle of a big smile. She shook hands with us.

'I've heard such a lot about you both. Did you get the younger ones fixed up all right?' I nodded. I was too shy to speak. She said, 'Good for you, your mama said you were a wonderful manager. Now come on in. Lunch is nearly ready. We're all going to eat together.' I couldn't believe this. I'd never dreamt of eating a meal with a white person in their house.

Just as we were going in the door, Sharky came running back from barking after the taxi. He rushed straight to Welly and panted up at him.

Madam said, 'Oh, look, Welly! Sharky likes you. Go on, pat him – he's a bit sad because Mrs Bailey went off and left him.' Welly didn't believe this great dog could want to be friends with him but he did pat his head, kind of nervously.

The Big House wasn't big, it was *huge*. There was hardly any furniture, which made it look bigger. Mrs Bailey had sold everything except one little bed and a table and chairs. Madam – she tried to get us to call her Pauline, but I couldn't – said she was camping till her stuff came from England. I noticed there were ashtrays everywhere.

Outside was a beautiful big garden full of flowers, and a swimming pool shaped like a peanut shell. Madam saw us looking at it and said, 'Would you like a swim before lunch? Go on, go in in your *broeks*, nobody'll look.' I shook my head as if I was trying to shake it off, but Welly opened his mouth finally and said, 'I will.'

We went back in the house, and two minutes later we heard a big splash as Welly jumped in in his underpants. Sharky ran around the edge of the pool as if he'd like to jump in too. I was scared my brother might drown, but he didn't. He threshed around and ducked under the water and charged back and forth across the pool where it wasn't deep. I wished I'd had the courage to go in! I went into the kitchen to help Amayi.

But Madam was in there helping, too! So we didn't have a chance to talk till after lunch. At table Amayi kept very quiet and let Madam talk to us. She asked us a lot of questions, mainly about school, and about the other kids at home. Then she dropped her bombshell.

'I want you all to come and live here in Harare with your mama.'

Welly and I looked at each other. We didn't know what to think, let alone say. But it stopped us eating, just the impossible idea of leaving home and living here. How could anything like that possibly happen? Black people who worked for whites in the city *never* had their kids to live with them.

'But that can't happen all at once. The building your mama lives in is too small, and there's a lot of work needs doing. I think it's awful, the way she's been living, but we're going to change all that.'

We didn't talk at all. We just looked down at our plates.

After lunch we helped Amayi clear the dishes and wash them up in the big modern kitchen. Madam left us alone, and at last we could talk.

I'd never seen Amayi so excited. She could hardly hold herself in.

'Madam is an angel,' she began. 'She's from South Africa but she went to England a long time ago because she tried to help black people, so the South African government sent her away.

'When she got here, she was sick. When I found her she was just fell on the bed. She had fever. I didn't know what to do. She looked so bad I called in the lady from next door, and she called a doctor. When Madam got better she told me, if I hadn't been there she might've died. But then she said she didn't want a black servant. In England she did everything for herself.

'I thought she was going to fire me. I was so scared I cried. She made me sit down like real people and we talked. She asked me all about myself and then she looked at the hut. She said, "Well, if you are going to stay, I can't have you living like this." Then she started talking about you coming to live with me, and Welly going to a private school in the city.'

I didn't say anything. Nor did Welly. It was all too much to take in. Sharky was in the kitchen with us. He was acting like he was Welly's dog and Welly was much braver with him now. Welly *always* wanted a dog.

As for me, I was all upset in my head.

Madam and Amayi took us to look at the hut. It was just one room. Madam was telling us how it was going to be made bigger. She said she was going to help Amayi in other ways. She was going to teach her better cooking, and how to sew.

'I know your mama can't read or write, and maybe we can do something about that, too, but the important thing is that at least one of you children should get an education. If you'd been the oldest, Crystal, it would be you, because girls should be educated just like boys, but I can only afford to send one of you. That's the best way I can help you to help her.'

'Welly can read,' I said.

'There's more to education than just reading,' Madam said. She said that like a real white person. Like she expected to get her own way.

Madam let us stay the night in the Big House, sleeping on folded blankets on the floor. Before we went to sleep I said to Welly, 'What do you think?' He said, 'What's there to think about?' I thought, *He wants to come now*. But I didn't.

Maybe the new madam was some kind of angel, and this was like heaven for sure. But you don't want to go to heaven till you die. It wasn't like a real place. Our house was home. I'd got used to running things and looking after the little ones. I didn't want everything to change. And I felt as if Madam was stealing Welly.

In the morning Amayi cooked bacon and eggs and we all ate breakfast together. Madam talked more. She talked about how Zim was going to be a good country with lots of prosperity, and blacks and whites sharing as equals. It wasn't right yet, she said, but she wanted to help it come right, and that was part of why she wanted to help us.

Amayi didn't say a thing. She kept nodding and smiling at us.

Madam took me to the bus station. Welly was staying. He had to start school straight away. She gave me some money and put me on the bus. All the black people in the bus were looking at us. Especially when she kissed me.

She said, 'See you soon! Your mama will be home next weekend and she'll tell you what's the next step in my Master Plan.' Then she smiled and waved and the bus left.

All the way back I thought about how strange and lonely I felt without Welly. I made up my mind that I wasn't going along with Pauline's 'master plan', whatever that meant. I wanted to keep things the way they were. Not to let her take over our lives. I was *determined*.

But it came out quite different.

When Amayi came for the next visit, she said it was fixed. Welly had already started school – with all new clothes Madam bought him – and I was to come with the other kids as soon as the hut was ready. Amayi had no idea how I felt, till I said No.

I was ready for a big argument and I started explaining, but Amayi just looked at me as if she'd never seen me before. She wouldn't listen or talk to me. She just talked to the others about how nice it was in Harare with the new madam. She said Welly had a new bicycle . . . Jeena had crept into Amayi's arms. The boys were jumping up and down. I couldn't stand it. I cracked right away and promised to go along with the master plan when the time came. And I did.

We lived, all of us, in the hut (which had three rooms now, floor, ceiling, electricity, proper plumbing, a TV and everything) for exactly two weeks before Madam woke us one morning to ask why the electric gate was open, and where Sharky was . . .

Welly'd left a note for Amayi that I had to read to her, but it didn't say much. I was the only one who had a clue how he hated that school, where even the black kids, who had rich fathers, called him son-of-a-cleaning-woman, and how he missed his friends in the Township. Not that he ever got back there. Sharky came back alone. Madam did all she could to find him, but it was no good. I think he just got lost in the city. He was only just twelve.

Madam dried her tears and said, 'Right, Crystal, you go in there and show 'em what a woman can do.' And she sent me to the good school. I fought to stay home with the kids, but she wouldn't listen, and Amayi backed her up.

It was the best thing that could have happened to me. Sixteen years later I can admit it.

When Madam was dying, which she did because of smoking, she said, 'Well, Crys, wasn't I right?' She hadn't forgotten how I'd been against it. I turned on her oxygen and said 'Yes,' and I didn't add that she wasn't so right about Zim.

I could look after Amayi now I've got a good job, but Amayi won't leave the hut. She stayed on after Pauline died, to work for the new madam, just because she thinks Welly might show up one day. The new madam's black, she's the wife of a government minister. And she's never told Amayi to call her by her first name.

This is Not a Fairy Tale

by Jeremy Strong
(UNITED KINGDOM)
illustrated by Nick Sharratt

This is something that happened a long time ago, before people knew what was real and what wasn't – though they thought they knew the difference. It was a time when bears and wolves roamed the countryside, when there were trolls and goblins, dwarves and unicorns, dragons and witches and wicked stepmothers and proud queens who were not as beautiful as Snow White, and so on. You get the picture.

Luke was a young man of eighteen. He was good-looking, but very poor. His father had died when a pig fell on him. (That was the sort of accidental death people had in those days. Luke's grandmother had been mown down by a flock of runaway chickens.) Luke was only six when his father died, and after that he was brought up by his mother, Old Crone, and his pet dog, Shaggy. There was little work to be found in the ramshackle village where Luke lived and because there was little work, there was no money to be made. Luke muddled along as best he could. He was happy to turn his hand to anything, so he did a bit of wood-chopping here and a bit of shepherding there and so on. In this way he just about managed to keep himself fed, although his clothes would certainly not have won any fashion prizes. They were torn and tattered and dirty.

Luke did, however, have one big advantage despite his humble environment. He had a brain, and Luke's brain was a good brain and he used it for doing what brains do best of all — thinking. He used to listen to what all the wise old villagers chatted about during the long dark evenings. He would lap up every word. He would listen to their old tales, enthralled.

The old villagers were very proud of their wisdom. They sat round a winter fire and said things like: 'We be wise old villagers. What I say is, before the last apple falls, there'll be trouble.'

And all the other elders of the village would go: 'Ooh, ahh, Old Jezebel, she be right there. Before the last apple falls, there'll be trouble!'

And then someone else might say: 'Ah, but when the moon is red and the hawthorn is in bloom, that's the time to be darning socks!' And they would all nod their heads in agreement.

Now it just so happened that Luke was a great reader. He wanted to know everything about the world around him, and sometimes he even allowed people to pay him with books rather than money. Luke had already learned a great deal from books, and what he had learned made him think that most of the old wisdom spouted by the ancient crones in the village was a big load of nonsense. He worked out that if he lived his life based on the things the elders told him he would never get anything done at all. He certainly was not going to wait for a red moon and blooming hawthorn before he set about darning his socks. He decided to use his brain instead.

Now, it so happened that there was a lot of talk in the village about the local princess. Her name was Ramona and she lived at the top of the mountain. (The village was at the bottom.) It was said that Ramona had flaming red hair and was as beautiful as the sunset. Very few people had actually seen the princess because she had never come down from the mountain, and they had never been up it. The only way people knew about her was because occasionally messages were sent down from the castle. They were written on paper, folded into darts and launched over the battlements.

Ramona was due for marriage, but despite the best efforts of her parents, no suitable husband could be found. The rules for marriage were the usual weird rules that people used in those days. The prospective suitor had to climb the mountain from bottom to top and then he could claim the hand of the gorgeous Ramona. Now climbing a mountain doesn't sound especially difficult, and you would be right to think that actually climbing the mountain – the climbing bit itself – was not terribly hard. No, the awkward bit was what might happen on the way. You see, as you went up the mountain you would quite likely meet with the Black Bear. If you didn't see him you would no doubt come across the Trolls of Tiddly Crag, or the Waggletooth Witch. Then there were the Wild Wolves of Black Fen, the Dragon of Doom and the most frightening thing of all – the Giant Man-Eating Unicorn That Nobody Had Ever Seen. So all the suitors died on their way up, and this was also why Ramona never came down from the castle and all messages were sent down by paper dart. (You may wish to know how the villagers got messages up to the castle and the short answer is, they didn't. They had yet to invent a dart that could be flung that high.)

Now Luke was not only bright, he was also adventurous. Nowadays he would have gone white-water rafting and bungee jumping, but nobody had heard of such things in those days, so he didn't. But he did want to see the world. He wanted to escape from the humdrum little village where half of the elders spouted nonsense. He wanted to travel, but he didn't want to do it by himself. He wanted a companion. So it was that his thoughts turned towards the Princess Ramona.

Luke knew all about the dreadful creatures that haunted the mountain, yet he was still determined to see if he could win the hand of the beautiful Princess Ramona in marriage. He sat down and had a long, hard think. Then he got up and packed his bag. He put in some fruit and a salami sausage for the journey, because he didn't know how long it would take, and he set off up the mountain.

As he left the village the elders shouted after him, 'If you see the Waggletooth Witch you must cross your fingers behind your back and run like the wind and shout out the alphabet backwards!'

Some of them offered this advice too: 'When the Black Bear tries to eat you, rub your skin with acorn juice and hiss. Then the bear will vanish.'

Even his mother had wise words for him. 'Trolls love to dance. If you come across them you must play your magic violin and they will dance and dance until they drop down dead.'

'Right,' nodded Luke. He told everyone that he would certainly bear in mind their advice, and he set off. He had not got far before he came across a patch of brambles as big as Europe. The brambles were thick and tall and covered in sharp, flesh-tearing thorns. What made them worse was that here and there he could see bits of torn clothing left behind by some of the princes who had tried to find a way through. There were even a few skeletons hanging around. They didn't look very happy.

Luke looked at the brambles and he thought for a bit and then he made himself a small fire. He found two nice bits of thick wood and pushed their ends into the fire and waited until they had caught the flame nicely. Armed with these flaming brands Luke advanced on the brambles. They sizzled and hissed and spat and curled up and shrivelled at the heat from the flames and so, bit by bit, Luke made his way through the brambles, leaving a nice clean charred path behind him, ready for his return.

Luke pressed on up the mountain, whistling. All of a sudden out popped the Waggletooth Witch. She was hairy, she was horrid. She was the ugliest thing Luke had ever laid eyes on. Her nose was like a giant parrot's beak, but covered with warts and pimples and sprouting hairs. Did Luke cross his fingers behind his back and run away saying the alphabet backwards? No.

'I'm going to put a nasty spell on you!' cackled the witch.

'Why's that?' asked Luke, quite reasonably.

'Because I am so hideous and you are so handsome I cannot bear the sight of you.' And the witch reached into her handbag and pulled out her wicked witch's wand.

'I don't know why you say you are hideous,' said Luke calmly, because he had once read in a book that a little kindness can go a long way. 'I think you are extraordinary.'

The witch, who was just in the process of making all the right sort of wavy movements with her wand before casting the spell, stopped in mid wave. 'What? Why do you say that?'

Luke boldly stepped forward. He didn't want to show how frightened he was. 'Oh yes, you really are quite extraordinary. I have never seen a nose like yours. It is unique. It is wonderful – an empress in the world of noses.'

The Waggletooth Witch blushed. She did! She turned pink and then red and then back to pink. She fluttered her eyelashes. 'Oh you! You're just saying that!'

'It's true,' said Luke.

'Ah, well I am not sure I believe you,' said the Waggletooth Witch with a cunning leer. 'I bet you wouldn't dare kiss me.'

Luke smiled. (Behind the smile his teeth were firmly gritted.) 'I thought you'd never ask,' he said, and he gave the witch a stonking kiss.

To say that the Waggletooth Witch was amazed would be an understatement. She staggered back, quite delighted. Nobody had ever kissed her before, not even her own mother when she was a child. 'What a perfect gentleman you are. Nobody has ever done that for me. I wish you luck on your journey.'

So Luke carried on up the mountain and he had hardly gone any distance when the bushes parted and out sprang the Black Bear. Did Luke rub himself with acorn juice and hiss? No, he didn't.

'Grrrr,' said the bear, in a bear-ish sort of way. 'What are you doing halfway up this mountain?'

'I have come to seek the hand of the Princess Ramona,' explained Luke.

'Oh really? Do you know how many princes I have eaten?'

'No, I don't,' Luke answered truthfully.

'Thirty-two,' said the bear, also truthfully.

'Then you must have been very hungry,' Luke replied, and that stopped the bear in his tracks. The bear had never heard the like. Of course he had been hungry. That was why he ate all the princes. This young man was evidently very wise.

Luke sat down at the bear's feet and patted the grass beside him. 'In my bag I have some salami. Would you like some?'

'What is salami?' asked the bear, sitting down and gazing at Luke with great curiosity.

Luke got out the salami sausage and he let the bear smell it. Then he cut off a big chunk and gave it to the bear. The bear ate the salami and licked his lips and said he thought that salami sausage was a lot nicer than princes, and a lot less bony. Then he wished Luke good luck with his journey and hoped that they would meet again.

Luke carried on up the mountain and before long he came face to face with the Trolls of Tiddly Crag. 'What a busy day I'm having,' thought Luke. The trolls surrounded Luke and danced round him chanting horrible things. They were short, ugly little creatures, with needle-sharp teeth and a taste for human flesh. Now they bared their teeth and pulled horrible faces at Luke.

Did Luke pull out his magic violin and make them dance until they all dropped down dead? Of course not. He didn't have a magic violin and he didn't know how to play the violin even if he did have one.

Instead he just stood there and laughed. 'You're so cute!' he told the trolls.

'No we're not. We're horrible!' yelled the Chief Troll.

'But you're so cuddly,' insisted Luke, giving them such a big smile.

'Shut up!' roared the Chief Troll. 'We're horrible, horrible, horrible!'

Luke shook his head and repeated quietly, 'Cute!'

'Aargh!' screamed the Chief Troll. 'We are horrible!' and he flew into such a rage that he exploded on the spot. BANG! The other trolls ran away, terrified that the same fate awaited them.

By this time Luke had reached the top of the mountain and he walked into the castle and found the Princess Ramona, who was every bit as beautiful as everyone had said.

'Great heavens above,' cried Ramona, 'someone has actually made it to the top of the mountain and he's rather gorgeous, despite the totally untrendy clothes and strong smell of garlic.'

For the sake of decency and so on, I am going to leave out the bit where they fall in love and have a smooch, but they did all that and then Luke said it was time to go back down the mountain.

'But I can't,' said Ramona. 'There's a Waggletooth Witch down there, and a bear and trolls and all sorts of horrible creatures and brambles and I might tear my dress.'

'We can't stay up here forever,' said Luke. 'Down there, at the bottom of the mountain, that is where the rest of the world starts, and there is so much to see and to do and I am going to see it and do it and I want you to be with me.'

'I dearly want to see the rest of the world,' murmured Ramona. 'And I want to be with you more than anything else.'

But Ramona was very frightened and she would not go down the mountain. Luke eventually set off on his own. 'I shall wait for one day,' he told her. 'After that I shall set off on my own if you have not arrived. You must make up your mind, Ramona. You must overcome your own fear. I cannot do that for you.'

Halfway down the mountain Luke met the trolls again. 'Cute,' he smiled, and this time they hid under rocks before any more of them could explode. He met the Black Bear, but the salami was finished so he gave the bear a salad sandwich instead. 'Hmmm, nice,' said the bear. 'People often forget that bears are omnivores. I love eating greens.'

Next up was the Waggletooth Witch, who simply blushed and smiled and fluttered her eyelashes. Luke got away with blowing her a kiss, and after that he reached the bottom of the mountain without any further problems. He never did see The Giant Man-Eating Unicorn That Nobody Had Ever Seen, which didn't surprise Luke, but did surprise all the villagers when they asked what had happened.

Meanwhile, on top of the mountain, Ramona gazed back down towards the village. And she wondered. Did she dare? She desperately wanted to be with Luke and to explore the world and escape from her horrible castle. But was her love strong enough to overcome her fears? And, if she did overcome her fears and set off down the mountain, how would she deal with the Waggletooth Witch and the trolls and the bear and the brambles? Would she be as wise and kind as Luke?

You see, this story does not have a fairy-tale ending, because it isn't a fairy tale. In real life there are always problems, and you have to solve them.

THE END

Epilogue

Why isn't this a fairy tale? Because it hasn't got any fairies in it. In fact, do you know ANY fairy tales that have got fairies in them?

Whose Hair is it Anyway?

by Beverley Naidoo
(SOUTH AFRICA)

illustrated by Emily Bolam

I have always wanted to try my hand at hairdressing – for real, I mean. When I was six I got Mum to give me one of those doll's heads from Santa – you know the sort, with long nylon hair, cute little spiky curlers and a pink plastic hairdryer. (Of course I had found out about Santa by then but I didn't let on 'cause Mum used to give me a present from her and Dad as well.) I would spend hours fiddling with Sophie's hair. I called her Sophie because I overheard Mum talking about how 'sophisticated' children were nowadays and I thought it sounded really grown-up. Anyway, all my other dolls had names, so why shouldn't Sophie? Just because she only had a head, it didn't mean she hadn't got feelings, did it?

But playing with Sophie's hair wasn't like doing the real thing. Gradually I got bored with pretending I was 'Julie' or 'Rachel' – a top stylist at Watford's top salon – and Sophie was left on my dressing table for months on end, her stare fixed on me through perfectly round blue eyes. Her hair gathered dust like everything else in my room between one 'Operation Clean-Up' and the next.

Much more fun than playing with Sophie, however, was getting my hands on proper hair. My best time was when we were going to Ireland. I was only about seven at the time and I sat cramped in the back seat with Mum and my brother, while our friends, Maureen and her husband, drove us. Maureen has really long hair, which she let hang over her seat just in front of me. It was the same reddish colour as Sophie's but more natural — and she let me brush it, all the way to Ireland! Well, nearly all the way before we got on the boat. Every now and then she would ask for a little rest and I would sit untangling the fine strands of hair from the brush until she was ready to let me start again.

Sometimes I also used to get a chance to try out plaits and different styles on some of my friends with long hair during storytime at school. That was when we were a lot younger and used to sit on a mat in the story corner. The best place to be was at the far side of the teacher, so she could only really see you if she had sideways eyes like a squirrel, or if she turned her head. I'm saying 'she' because all the teachers in the infants and lower juniors were women. It's funny, but the only two men teachers always seemed to stick with the older children. Maybe they thought we needed people like mummies when we were little more than people like daddies. Mind you when Mum gets mad, I can tell you I need my dad!

I could also have done with my dad for protection the

day the teacher caught me making Sarah turn her head so I could plait the last strands above her left ear. Somehow I had got carried away after making six plaits around the back of her head, neatly finished off with blue elastic bands (brought from home) and matching beads (borrowed from the bead tin in the maths tray). It was a brilliant story, too, that she interrupted, just to tell me off, all about a girl called Rapunzel.

But on the whole, fiddling with other people's hair doesn't cause any major problems. It's like knitting – you can unpick and start again. Perhaps that has been the fascination for me, the idea of endless possibility. Now cutting . . . that's another matter. It's not that hair won't regrow, but at the point when you actually snip the scissors together and see a loop of hair tumble off, there's something final about it. I cried after my first and only attempt at giving Sophie a new look. I guessed I was going to go wrong after I had taken the first small snip with Mum's nail scissors. But I could see I had to go on and, although I didn't take very much off, by the time I had finished, she was never again to be the perfect model for a salon photograph.

I am still puzzled about why on earth I tried cutting my own hair. It was two years ago, when I was nine. Perhaps I was suffering from not being able to play with my friends' hair so much. We no longer had stories on a mat in the corner and there just weren't so many opportunities. After our class went swimming I could offer to help a friend with long hair, but dealing with tangled damp hair isn't quite the same, especially with Mrs Masters yelling at you to hurry up. The atmosphere wasn't the same any more.

I think I must have been in a bad or mad mood that day, because I loved my thick dark hair being so long and being able to do different things with it. In fact, when Mum used to get irritated because I was spending hours sorting out my hair instead of getting ready for school, she would say, 'We really should get your hair cut!' But I would protest loudly, 'No you won't! It's *my* hair!'

All I can remember when I went mad with the scissors on my own hair, was a sense of power. Funny to have power over your own hair and yourself! It was long enough for me to hold thick batches of it out sideways and watch it in the mirror as I tried to add a professional look to my scissor movement. It fell in thick chunks; I studied the new me. Who was that person in the mirror?

Mum's first reaction was, 'Oh my God! What have you done?'

Dad, on the other hand, immediately found the whole affair a joke. 'What are you complaining about?' he said to Mum. 'You wanted her to have it short! It's only a bit wonky!'

He must have seen the tears welling up in my eyes. I obviously wasn't in control that day after all. He put his arm around me.

'Don't worry, my darling! It'll grow again!'

A real philosopher is my dad.

So what possessed me to offer to cut Gemma's hair yesterday? I can't say it was a spur of the moment decision. Kathy, Lizzie, Gemma and I have been into 'hair talk' for ages at school. It's not that we don't chat about lots of other things, of course we do. But it's something we've got in common — until yesterday.

The idea must have been growing in my mind ever since Gemma had started saying that she wanted to have her hair cut, but her mum said no, she couldn't afford to take her to the hairdresser. I felt really sorry for her. But I don't think I realized that the little speck of an idea was getting bigger and stronger until one day, Pow!

'Why don't we all meet up at my house on Sunday and we can do each other's hair? I can cut yours for you, Gemma, if you like.'

Everyone thought it was a terrific plan. I only had to persuade Mum to let me have my friends round, and that wasn't difficult. I promised we wouldn't make any noise to disturb her work and she said it would be fine as long as she didn't have to go out for a meeting. By Saturday she confirmed it was OK, so I got Dad to take me to the shops to buy some drink and crisps for the occasion. I didn't say anything to Mum about the hair session. I'm not sure why. Maybe I just didn't think it was anything to do with her... you know the way you think some things are just between you and your friends.

We had a great time – choice music from my albums, food, drink, Kathy's new shampoo, Gemma's pink ringlet curling sticks (for me to try out) and Mum's razor-sharp hair scissors. We shut the door, although Mum and Dad were very considerate, getting on with their own things and letting us get on with enjoying ourselves.

Gemma, seated in front of the dressing-table mirror, said she wanted four inches off, so I set to work. Her hair is very curly so it certainly wasn't a matter of just cutting straight. She was smiling and giggling and in fact we were all pretty happy. Only when I was about halfway through my creation, did Gemma introduce a slightly worrying note.

'Oh dear! What if my mum is cross? Perhaps she really doesn't want me to get my hair cut.'

I don't think my mum had even noticed that Gemma's hair had been shortened when she came upstairs to tell Gemma her Dad was waiting outside. She noticed our hair was wet though.

'Goodness! Have you all been washing your hair?'

'Yes, it's rather a weird thing to do when you go visiting, isn't it!' laughed Kathy, standing in front of the bedroom door so Mum wouldn't come in.

I was very pleased with the ringlet effect from Gemma's curlers, that is, until my brother called me Medusa and mentioned snakes. Don't brothers somehow have a knack of ruining things? That was the one picture

in my book of legends that really gave me nightmares — all those twisted snakes crawling out of the monster-woman's head. But, on the whole, it had been a good day. Gemma and the others had liked the final result of my handiwork. I might even have tried out the ringlet curlers overnight for extra effect, if it hadn't been for the Medusa comment. Drifting off into a pleasurable semi-dream in bed, recreating highlights of the day, I was only vaguely aware of the phone ringing and Mum answering it.

Mum called me into her study first thing this morning.

'Do you know who rang last night?'

It had been Gemma's dad. He said that his wife was too furious to speak, so he was ringing for her. My mum was totally taken by surprise because he asked if she knew what we had been up to. Mum had to say no. So he told her. According to what he said, Gemma is not going to be allowed out to friends, and her mum thinks her hair is such a mess that she will have to take her to a hairdresser after all.

'But Mum,' I began to sob, 'that's why I offered to cut it ... because her mum had said they couldn't afford it.'

I didn't add any excuses to do with how much I love handling hair. I could see Mum was angry, too.

'Didn't you realize what could happen? Do you really think Gemma's mum will ever let her come and visit you again?'

*

It is as if life has come tumbling down on me ... just like the flock of Gemma's golden hair. Mum has seen it now. I feel so sorry for Gemma, and so sorry for myself that I can't stop crying. I have just written a letter to Gemma's parents saying it was all my fault and I am sending them a cheque from my mum to pay for the hairdresser. I'm going to pay Mum back from my pocket money.

I shall have to stop crying because I have to go to school. I only hope Gemma isn't mad at me now. I know I shouldn't have done it, because look at the trouble we are in. But, you know, there is still one question which keeps going round and round in my mind. I can't get rid of it. Whose hair is it anyway?

PS You'll never guess what happened at school today. Lots of people came up to me and said, 'Rukhsana! You're a brilliant haircutter!'

In fact three girls are going home to ask their mums if I can cut their hair! However, perhaps they had better ask their dads first. Gemma told me that her mum actually quite liked what I had done, but it was her dad who hit the roof!

Does *that* answer my question?

Author's note: When my daughter Maya was Rukhsana's age, she really did cut a friend's hair, with the same consequences! I wrote this story the next day to calm down.

Up River

by Rosina Umelo
(NIGERIA)
illustrated by Karin Littlewood

It happened because everyone was busy.

Usually Ada and Ngozi stayed with neighbours while their parents went to meetings. But that day ... sorry, everyone was busy ... nobody could help.

'So we'll take them with us for once,' Mama said. 'No problem. The Secretary will find somewhere to put them.'

Ada didn't mind. She was quite bored with staying with the same neighbours so often and was ready for a change. Ngozi didn't care. They all knew she'd fall asleep in the car as she always did. Ada preferred to look out at people in the busy streets, particularly when they were going to somewhere new.

Too soon for her, they arrived at the gates of a large and important building. 'Where are we?'

'At the meeting,' they said, as if that was the answer.

Inside the building everything was the same large size – steps, tables, chairs, mirrors.

'Oh, what a little darling!' someone said, pointing at Ngozi. This must be the Secretary, a large efficient lady. 'And she's asleep! What a good thing.'

Mama was explaining, 'We had to bring them. There was no one ... and we didn't want to miss the meeting.'

'Of course not! So why don't we put them in the library? They'll be nice and quiet there.'

And maybe you hope that I'm going to sleep too, Ada thought. *I knew it ... you think I'm a nuisance.*

The Secretary opened one of the tall doors and led the way. Ada had never seen such a huge room. It was full of books: on shelves, in locked glass-fronted bookcases and special displays. A row of windows along one wall was draped with long, green velvet curtains, all braids and tassels. They stretched from the polished floor up to the ceiling. And that was white and decorated with twirls and flowers and shells like the top of a very expensive wedding cake. The room was very much bigger than the Public Library and the books were quite different. There, they were brightly coloured and the covers shouted their names for everyone to hear. It was a noisy place. Here, they kept their names to themselves. They stood in rows, dark green, dark red, or brown. The golden titles were too faded for anyone to read.

'Lovely!' Ada said. She liked the place very much.

'Glad you think so.' The Secretary helped her to scramble up on to a very big chair. It was padded, with a high back and wide padded arms. She pushed it close to the table. 'Now, let me find you a book ... something with pictures ...'

'I can read,' Ada told her.

'Of course. But pictures ... a travel book perhaps.' The Secretary ran her hand over the faces of a row of tall books and pulled one down. She opened it in front of Ada on the table. 'There you are then!'

Where else can I be? Ada thought. Ngozi was lying asleep on a settee.

'You'll be all right,' Mama said. 'We're just along the corridor. We'll be back quite soon.' They went out. The room was very still.

Ada looked around and wondered whether to get down and explore the rest of the library. Later perhaps. I'd better take a look at this book first. It was very big; the page was the biggest she had ever seen and the picture was not quite a painting, not exactly a photograph. It showed a river, a rather dull stretch of water with foreign-looking trees. Then, when she looked at it more closely, she noticed that something strange was happening.

The picture was flowing off the page. And then it began to spread and spread all around her. The tall trees were above her. The big feathery fronds were slowly moving. She could hear the ripple and splash of water. She felt a bit dizzy and put out a hand to steady herself. She touched rough wood, not the smooth, padded arm of the chair or the silky, polished top of the table. She opened her eyes wide. She was sitting on a rough wooden seat in a boat. In front of her was a man, smoking an old pipe. A boy was steering the small craft.

Ngozi was sitting beside her. 'What's your name?'

'I'm Akpan ... because I'm the first son of my father. And this is Effiong.'

'Born on a Friday,' the boy explained.

'I'm Ngozi,' she told them. 'It means a blessing.'

'I hope you'll always give and get blessings,' Akpan said. Effiong grinned at her.

'My sister is Ada.'

'That's because I'm my parents' first daughter.' Ada thought she ought to join in the talk. No one seemed surprised that they were all in this place. Where could they be going? She looked at the green forest sliding past them. There was a strong river smell of mud and old leaves. It was not quiet: the air was full of humming, chirping, ringing sounds from all the busy insects and the frogs. Wherever they were going, they were not in a hurry. Behind the boat, two long lines spread out like a fan across the smooth still water. They carried little sparkles of sunlight under the trees. This river did not have green and grassy banks. Instead it spread into the forest and the trees came down to stand with their feet in the water. 'Where are we going?' she asked.

'Up river,' Akpan told her. 'We set fish traps two days ago. Be a blessing to us,' he smiled at Ngozi, 'and bring us a good catch.'

Effiong grinned again. He looked after the engine when it coughed and spluttered like an old man laughing at a good joke. Then it got its breath back and went smoothly, chugga, chugga.

Sometimes they passed bamboo houses built where the river moved into the land and the trees began. They stood on poles, like the stilt-walkers they had once watched at the carnival.

'Why?' Ngozi asked.

'The river is low now,' Akpan explained. 'But wait until the rainy season ... '

'Oh, I'm sorry but we can't stay so long,' Ada apologized. 'We're here while our parents are at a meeting.'

'Then I'll tell you, as you can't wait to see for yourselves. In the rainy season the river isn't quiet like this. It moves much faster. It gets very deep. It goes further into the forest. Everything is swampy or under water, but the houses sit above the flood ... well, usually they do.'

'What happens when the water gets too deep?'

'Then we get in our boats and move up river.'

'I've never seen so many trees,' Ada said, looking from side to side. Most were tall palm trees (she could see that now) with their feathery-looking tops. Other much taller trees looked down on everything. The sky was bright white, not blue. It was very hot. 'And does this river know where it's going?' It turned this way and that as if it couldn't make up its mind and seemed to turn as if to come back again.

'We know,' Akpan said comfortably. Putta putta putta, they chugged between the trees for a long time. Ngozi splashed the water with her hand. Then at last, 'Here we are. This is where we set our traps.'

Effiong turned the boat towards the side of the river. Here the land was a bit higher, and there was a sandy strip beside the water. 'We're going to be busy now so we'll have to leave you.'

Was it really white sand? Ada wondered. It was so smooth, it was almost shining, and it stretched in a straight line. 'What is that?' they both asked.

'The edge of the page,' Akpan said. 'Put out your hand and turn it, Ada. Goodbye!'

Ada put out her hand – felt silky, smooth wood – and looked up into her mother's smiling face.

'Well! You've both had a nice sleep!'

'I didn't ...' Ada began. But then how could she explain? 'Wait! Please wait!' But the Secretary busily closed the book and slipped it back among all the others. Ngozi sat up, yawned, and rubbed her eyes as she always did. The door was open. They could hear noisy people in the corridor, chatting, putting on coats, clattering down the steps. Car engines started up outside.

Ada slid down from the big chair. 'Thank you very much,' she said politely. No one was listening. Ngozi was waiting for her. She leaned forward and whispered, 'I do hope Akpan caught a lot of fish!'

The Dirty Dozen

by Tony Bradman
(UNITED KINGDOM)
illustrated by Daniel Postgate

When Robbie Jones rode into the park one summer Sunday morning and saw a team coming out of the pavilion, he knew it was love at first sight. He had always wanted to play in a real team, and he had seen lots before – but this was definitely the one for him.

They were kids of his own age, but they trotted towards the pitch in a line just like a Premiership side. Their green-and-black strip was pretty impressive, each player's shirt bearing a number *and* a name. They had a coach, too – a big, red-faced, tracksuited man with a very loud voice, who got them doing lots of professional-looking warm-up exercises. There were some dads on the touchline along with some mums and several little brothers and sisters. There was also an older man with a clipboard. Robbie left his bike by a tree and went over to ask him the team's name.

'Top Grove FC,' the man replied. 'They're playing Athletico Brockley. It's a pre-season friendly. Though I'm hoping it'll be a good game ... '

It wasn't. It was scrappy and unexciting, but Robbie didn't care. He was more interested in asking questions. Mr Clipboard was very helpful, and by the time the teams left the field – a scrambled goal gave Top Grove a 1–0 win – Robbie knew plenty about the team he wanted to join.

He knew, for instance, that they were playing in a new league, that Mr Clipboard was the league's secretary, that the big coach was a wealthy businessman called Mr Matthews and that his son Duncan was captain.

Robbie took a deep breath and headed for the Top Grove players.

'You were brilliant, Dunc!' Robbie heard somebody say, which was strange, thought Robbie, Duncan hadn't really had *that* good a game.

'Er ... hi,' said Robbie nervously. The group fell silent and turned to stare at him. 'I was just wondering if you needed any more players ... '

'What school do you go to?' said Duncan, stepping forward.

'Sunny Bank,' mumbled Robbie, his heart sinking.

'Really?' said Duncan. He glanced at Robbie's battered old bike, and then looked pointedly at Robbie's scuffed, non-label trainers. 'Actually, I think we've got all the players we need at the moment, haven't we, guys?'

Robbie heard somebody sniggering, and felt his cheeks burn. He trudged away, past Mr Matthews and

Mr Clipboard, who were arguing. Top Grove's opposition had pulled out of the next friendly: Mr Matthews wanted a replacement and Mr Clipboard couldn't find one.

Robbie rode out of the park. It wasn't fair, he thought. OK, so Duncan Matthews was posh and rich. But he could still have given him a chance.

Robbie brooded upstairs in his bedroom until Sunday lunch; and right through the meal; and afterwards while he sat in the front room between his mum and dad. Not that they noticed. They were busy arguing too.

'I'm fed up with you deciding what we watch on TV the whole time,' Mum was saying. 'If it isn't blasted men kicking a ball, it's blasted men running around shooting at each other. What *is* this rubbish anyway?'

'It's called *The Dirty Dozen*,' Dad replied with a heavy sigh. 'And according to the cable TV guide, it's a classic. This American officer leads a team of nutters on a special mission behind enemy lines. Got it?'

Mum wittered on, but Robbie wasn't listening any more. The film had given him an idea. A team on a special mission ... a dozen was a football team, plus substitute. A team in which *he* might play – and show Top Grove what he could do! Robbie sat forward suddenly, very excited.

'See?' said Dad triumphantly. 'Robbie thinks it's good.'

Robbie remembered the row between Mr Matthews

and Mr Clipboard – Top Grove didn't have any opponents next Sunday. Although they might *if* he could get a team together. He focused on the screen. The film's hero was talking to the kind of trusted second-in-command that heroes always have. A picture of his best friend instantly flashed into Robbie's head. 'Just popping out to see Gary,' he said, and jumped up.

'Traitor,' muttered Dad as Mum grabbed the remote.

Robbie rode to Gary's house. Gary's big brother Ian answered the door. 'All right, Robbie?' he growled. Ian had hit puberty in a big way, and his vocal chords had travelled so far south he sounded as though he should be doing voice-overs for horror movie trailers. 'You'll find him upstairs.'

Robbie paused on the landing by his friend's room. He suddenly felt uneasy. What was he going to tell Gary? Robbie wasn't the only one who wanted to play proper football. He realized Gary and his other mates did too. They hated the fact that Sunny Bank didn't have a team. Maybe *they* would like the chance to show Top Grove what they could do ...

Robbie was confident of his own ability – but why make things difficult? Why give himself lots of competition? He'd played football in the school playground with his mates for years, so he knew some of them could be pretty impressive. They might even look better than him on the day... No, it would be best to keep his plan secret, he thought. He could tell Gary this was a one-off, a single opportunity to play a proper game, but no more than that. Then, if the plan worked, he could simply act surprised.

So, for the second time that day, Robbie took a deep breath. He pushed open Gary's door. Gary turned to smile at him and Robbie experienced a slight, but definite, twinge of guilt. He almost managed to ignore it, too.

'I'm not sure, Robbie,' said Gary. 'Just suppose we *could* put a team together. Nobody we know has ever played a proper game, have they? I don't even have any proper boots. We'd probably get slaughtered.

'And who's actually going to phone this Mr Matthews to arrange the game?' he went on. 'He'll only want to talk to an adult. Mind you, I suppose we could always ask your dad. He likes football, doesn't he?'

'I'd rather not,' said Robbie hurriedly. 'And I, er ... think it's best if we don't involve our parents.'

Gary raised an eyebrow, then shrugged.

'We know someone who sounds like a grown-up, though,' Robbie added.

It didn't take much to persuade Ian — just a promise to get the phone number of a boy whose older sister Ian fancied. Then, after a search in the phone book, calls to the wrong Mr Matthews and a brief, loud conversation with the right one, the deed was done.

'There you go, lads,' said Ian. 'Kick-off ten-thirty next Sunday morning.'

'*Yes!*' said Robbie and raised a fist. He was on his way ...

*

Robbie and Gary rang their mates the next morning. Everybody was up for the game and Robbie soon had a list of twelve names, including his own and Gary's. Robbie decided to set up a training session, too. If the team did get slaughtered, he realized, *he* wouldn't be able to show his skills. So he'd need the lads to have a bit of basic organization, at least.

That Tuesday, Gary ticked everybody off the list as they arrived – Wayne, Lefty, Luke, Big Dan, Billy, Jez, Ahmed, Willsy, Darren and Martin. They were all excited and stood around chattering. Then the inevitable arguments started about who should play in what position. This was something Robbie hadn't bargained for. He simply assumed he'd play in central midfield, his dream spot. But now he realized that unless he took control of the situation, he could end up playing anywhere.

'Quiet!' he yelled. Everybody fell silent and stared at him. 'This was my idea, so I'm in charge, and *I'll* decide who plays where.' There was some grumbling, but it soon died down. 'Right, Luke, you're in goal ... '

It didn't take Robbie long to make his decisions. He knew everybody's strengths and weaknesses – who could head the ball, who could tackle. And, of course, he gave himself the position he wanted. He'd promised the lads a training session, so he set up a six-a-side game of attackers versus defenders, although it soon deteriorated into an aimless kickabout – which was OK by Robbie.

Gary, however, thought otherwise.

'You'll have to be a bit tougher with us in tomorrow's session, Robbie,' he said when they found themselves marking each other. 'I mean, this is fun, but we're not really making much progress as a team, are we?'

'Tomorrow's session?' said Robbie uneasily.

'Maybe we could go to the library on the way home and get out some of those coaching videos for ideas,' said Gary. 'And some books too.'

'I wasn't planning on us doing any more training,' said Robbie.

'You what?' said Gary. Then he laughed. 'You're joking, right?'

'Huh, can't fool you, can I, Gary?' said Robbie, and smiled stiffly.

So Robbie scheduled more sessions. They trained on Wednesday, on Thursday and on Friday. Thanks to Gary and his coaching videos and manuals, they were more organized too. They had a final session on Saturday morning, agreed to meet in the park at ten o'clock the next day, and went home.

Gary and Robbie rode their bikes together as far as Robbie's house.

'You know, Robbie, I've been thinking,' said Gary. 'It's funny how things turn out, isn't it? I mean, if you and I hadn't been made to sit next to each other in reception class, we might never have become friends.'

'No, I guess not,' said Robbie, wondering where this was leading.

'Then you wouldn't have asked me to play in this game,' continued Gary, 'and it could be the biggest, most exciting day of my life. So I just wanted to say ... thanks, Robbie. Thanks for being such a good mate.'

'Don't mention it,' said Robbie quietly. 'Please, *don't* mention it ... '

Gary gave him a puzzled look, then rode off down the street.

The next morning, Robbie got up, had breakfast, put his kit in a Tesco's bag, and cycled off through drizzly rain to the park with it dangling from his handlebars. The other lads soon arrived, and so did Mr Clipboard.

'I take it you're Top Grove's mysterious opponents,' he said, his eyes drifting over them and finally coming to rest on Robbie. 'Hold on, don't I know you? Oh, never mind. If you'll just point me towards your coach ... '

'Er ... he can't make it today, I'm afraid,' said Robbie. *Mostly because he doesn't actually exist*, he thought. 'We're looking after ourselves.'

'I see,' said Mr Clipboard. 'This is all very irregular. First your coach contacts Top Grove direct instead of me, as he should have done, and now I find out that he's not even here! Tell me, what's the *name* of your team?'

'Their coach didn't give me a name,' boomed a voice behind them. Mr Matthews had also arrived. 'To be frank, I don't care *what* they're called so long as they're changed and ready by ten-thirty. Can we get on with it?'

'I suppose so,' said Mr Clipboard crossly, much to Robbie's relief. 'Although there's no need to be so rude,' he muttered. 'This way, boys ... '

Mr Clipboard directed Robbie and his mates into the pavilion, and to a big room that had benches round the walls, with coathooks above. There was a lot of nervous laughter as they got changed, and a few jokes at the expense of Mr Matthews. Then it was time for Robbie to lead them out.

The rain had stopped, but as Robbie ran on to the pitch he noticed it was quite muddy. It seemed bigger somehow, too, and it was strange to see the same scene as last week from such a different angle. There were the dads and mums and little brothers and sisters standing on the touchline ... And there were the Top Grove players in their shiny black-and-green shirts, sniggering openly at him and the rest of the lads. Robbie glanced at his mates' scruffy kit – the different replica strips, the odd socks, the cheap or borrowed boots – realized why, and felt his cheeks burning again.

'Right, can I have the two captains, please?' somebody called out.

It was Mr Clipboard and, to Robbie's surprise, he had changed too, but into a proper referee's strip. Robbie trotted over to him in the centre circle, and so did Duncan Matthews.

Duncan stared at Robbie and then smirked. 'Well,

well,' he said. 'I wasn't expecting *you* back so soon. If you're this keen to show me what you can do, maybe I should give you a trial after all. On second thoughts, perhaps I should see you play a bit first.'

'What's he talking about, Robbie?' said Gary.

Robbie turned around. Gary was standing next to him, scowling fiercely. Robbie opened his mouth to speak, but just then Mr Clipboard started talking about the coin toss, and Robbie had to pay attention. Robbie lost the toss and Duncan chose to kick off. Mr Clipboard placed the ball on the centre spot, and the teams got into position for the start of the game.

'Listen, Gary ...' said Robbie, as he moved back into midfield.

'Spare me the excuses,' Gary snapped. 'I *knew* there was something funny about this. Not wanting to do any more training ... you set it all up so you could get into their team! Hah! Some friend *you* turned out to be.'

Mr Clipboard blew his whistle as Gary finished speaking, and the game began, which was just as well, thought Robbie. He didn't have a clue what to say. Gary had him bang to rights, and Robbie felt absolutely sick. He noticed Willsy and Ahmed and Jez scowling, so they must have heard too.

Then somebody barged past him, and he was sent flying.

'Whoops, sorry!' said Duncan. 'I hope I didn't wake you up ... '

Robbie never forgot that first half, his introduction to proper football on a proper pitch. It was a total nightmare. Top Grove were unlucky not to score from their very first attack. Duncan took a pass from a midfielder on the edge of the box. If he'd hit the ball better, Luke would have had no chance. But his shot skidded wide, and Robbie started breathing again.

There was no let-up, though, and soon Top Grove were all over Robbie and the lads like a rash. Shots rained in on Luke's goal, and Robbie was amazed none of them went in. He and his teammates simply couldn't seem to get any possession, and spent their whole time chasing Top Grove players. This is ridiculous, thought Robbie at last, and stopped running. He looked at his team. They were supposed to be playing 4-4-2, with Wayne, Big Dan, Billy and Lefty across the back, Willsy, Ahmed, Gary and himself across the middle, and Martin and Jez up front, with Darren as sub. But the team completely lost its shape – they were continually out of position and getting in each other's way. What a mess, thought Robbie.

And so far *he* had done nothing but miss tackles and fall over. He hadn't put in any good passes yet, or hit a decent shot. He'd hardly been in Top Grove's half, and Duncan just laughed when he was near him. There was another problem too. The whole team seemed to know what Gary had said, even Darren on the touchline, and they were all scowling.

Then, of course, the inevitable happened. As Robbie watched, a Top Grove attack built up on the right-hand side. He started running again as a Top Grove player put in a cross. Somebody got a head to it, the ball came down in the area and a second later ... was bobbling over the line. Top Grove had scored, and Duncan raised his arms to the sky in triumph.

'Great goal, Duncan!' bellowed Mr Matthews. 'Smashing goal!'

That's strange, thought Robbie. He was certain Duncan hadn't got the final touch. But everybody in the Top Grove team seemed happy to let him take the credit – and Robbie suddenly understood why. *They had to*. I bet Mr Matthews started the team for Duncan, he thought, and that was the price for getting your name on one of those shiny black-and-green shirts ...

In fact, as Jez lost the ball from the restart, Robbie realized that Top Grove FC probably existed because Duncan thought he was a good player and wanted to show off. He kept calling for the ball and doing tricks with it, and playing up to the touchline. But then, thought Robbie, he had no right to criticize. Wasn't that more or less what *he* had been intending to do? Instead of which he'd simply managed to upset his best friend and his other mates. He remembered the word Dad had used: *traitor*. And in the end, what had it all been for? Robbie saw Duncan bustling one of his own teammates off the ball and realized there could never be a place at

Top Grove FC for truly good players, or anybody who couldn't take orders.

So the whole thing had been a total waste of time and effort, Robbie thought bitterly. Worse than that, he'd made a real fool of himself.

A few moments later Mr Clipboard blew his whistle for half-time. Robbie's mates slowly gathered in the centre circle and stood in a tight huddle with their backs to him. Top Grove headed for the touchline.

'Well, *you* were pretty useless,' said Duncan as he walked past Robbie with his players. 'But then I always thought you would be. I mean, what can you expect from someone who goes to a school like Sunny Bank?' Robbie heard more sniggering as they walked away ... and suddenly he felt very angry. Who the hell did Duncan Matthews think he was, talking to him like that? What made him so special? A father with enough money to *buy* him a team? It was time to take Duncan Matthews down a peg or two, he thought. Robbie turned and marched off towards his teammates.

'You all right, son?' said Mr Clipboard as Robbie went by him.

'I'm *fine*,' said Robbie grimly from between gritted teeth.

'Second half kicks off in five minutes,' said Mr Clipboard.

Robbie didn't reply. He kept on walking and finally stopped near his mates. The huddle opened to reveal Gary at its heart. Ten pairs of stern, disapproving eyes glared fiercely at Robbie, and none of his friends spoke.

'I know what you're thinking,' said Robbie, 'and you've got every reason to hate me. I *did* set this whole thing up to get into Top Grove, and I'm really sorry. You're my mates, and I realize now I'd much rather play with you than those creeps, OK? Even if it's only for one last half. So let's get out there and show them what the lads from Sunny Bank can *really* do.'

He didn't give them a chance to argue. He turned round and walked quickly towards the goal they'd be defending, and stood there kicking at the penalty spot. He noticed Mr Clipboard giving him a curious look, and also saw his mates talking to each other and occasionally glancing in his direction. Eventually Mr Clipboard called for the second half to begin.

For a moment Robbie thought his mates weren't going to play . . . but the huddle broke up and they drifted to their positions, Darren coming on for Billy, as they'd decided. Top Grove were ready, too. Mr Clipboard blew his whistle, and Jez tapped the ball to Martin. A Top Grove player came in for a tackle, and the ball squirted out to Duncan, who was smirking.

But this half it's going to be different, thought Robbie, streaking up to put in a tackle of his own. He swept the ball from Duncan's toes and surged beyond him. Duncan went down and appealed to the referee.

'No foul!' yelled Mr Clipboard, waving his arms. 'Play on!'

Robbie was on the edge of the Top Grove box now, their midfielders chasing him, their defenders looking nervous. He jigged past one, then laid the ball off to Martin, who thumped in a shot. The goalie smothered it.

'Keep your shape when they come forward, lads!' Robbie turned and yelled as the goalie rolled the ball to the nearest defender. He noticed with pleasure that Duncan wasn't smirking any more. 'Keep ... your ... shape!'

They did, too, mostly because Robbie kept reminding them. Fuelled by anger, he tore all over the pitch, getting in tackles, continually harassing, pressuring the Top

Grove players' first touch, encouraging his mates. They responded, too. They started talking to each other, calling for passes or cover, and making good runs off the ball when the team was in possession.

Top Grove didn't know what had hit them, and Robbie began to realize just how useful the training sessions and Gary's videos and manuals had been. The breakthrough must come soon, Robbie thought... and then it did.

Big Dan collected the ball in defence and hit it to Ahmed. He took it down the left-hand side into the corner and then turned in sharply, easily beating a defender, and drove the ball hard and low into the box.

Robbie had timed to perfection his run from midfield, appeared suddenly in the crowded area, and met the cross sweetly on the half volley. One all.

Robbie didn't celebrate, but turned round to go back for Top Grove's restart – and was promptly flattened by all his teammates, who rushed up to mob him. All of them, that is, except Gary, Robbie noticed.

Their second goal came pretty quickly. Mr Matthews was bellowing at his team so much that they started to get desperate, and eventually Duncan brought Jez down on the edge of the box. Mr Clipboard gave a free kick. Willsy blasted a shot into the wall, the ball rebounded to Robbie, and from fully twenty-five yards he curled it round the leaping keeper into the net. 2–1.

But it wasn't the best moment. That came right at the end.

Wayne knocked a long ball up to Willsy, who flicked it on first time to Robbie. He looked round and saw Duncan steaming in to close him down. Robbie waited, nutmegged him, and headed for the goal. Gary raced in from midfield beside him. Robbie dummied one defender, then a second, and only had the keeper to beat for a hat-trick. Now that *would* be something…

He knew he could do it, too. But he drew the keeper instead and neatly laid the ball off for his best friend to score with a simple tap-in. 3–1 – and this time Gary was the first in the mob that rushed to flatten Robbie.

'I take it this means I'm forgiven,' Robbie said

happily at last.

'Forgiven for what, exactly?' said Gary, grinning at him.

Robbie grinned back, and just then Mr Clipboard blew three blasts on his whistle for full-time. A ragged cheer went up from Robbie's mates, and he and Gary joined in, they high-fived each other with a loud '*Yes!*'

Duncan and his team slunk away to a *very* red-faced Mr Matthews.

'Could I have a word, lads?' called out Mr Clipboard, jogging over. 'I thought your second-half performance was terrific. You're just the kind of team we want in the league, so I was wondering – would you like to join?'

'Well, I er ... ' Robbie mumbled.

'Look, I've already guessed you don't really have a coach, but that doesn't matter,' said Mr Clipboard. 'I'll find you one, and a sponsor as well – if you promise to play like that against Top Grove a couple of times a season. It'll be worth it just to keep old Matthews quiet. Is it a deal?'

'It most definitely is!' said Robbie. Gary was nodding eagerly too.

'Good,' said Mr Clipboard. 'Here's my card – get your parents to give me a call tomorrow so we can set things in motion. Oh, and I *will* need a name for your team if I'm to plan your league fixtures. What's it to be?'

Robbie thought for a second. Sunny Bank United? Council Estate FC? No ... Then he looked at his victorious teammates. Their scruffy kit was covered in mud, and they were laughing and capering crazily for sheer joy.

'You can call us … The Dirty Dozen,' he said, and smiled.

It just seemed right, somehow.

Waiting for the Bus

by Adèle Geras
(UNITED KINGDOM)

illustrated by Korky Paul

Every day after school, I have to wait about fifteen minutes for the bus to take me home. Trust my mum and dad to buy a house on a road that you can only get to on the 196. Everyone else in my class arrives home ages before I do and sometimes I feel this is most unfair. But there are days when I'm glad that I do wait at that bus stop, and those days are the ones when Benson's there as well. Benson's real name is George Hedges (get it?) but he thinks Benson is classier. He doesn't reckon much to George.

'There's all kinds of famous Georges,' I told him the very first time I met him. 'All those kings and George Washington. Even George Michael.'

'Maybe that's it,' he said. 'Maybe there's too many of them. It's too common, that's what it is. Benson's more distinguished.'

He did a little tap dance around the litter bin and continued: 'You call me Benson.'

He's been turning up at the bus stop every few days

for the last couple of months. It's hard to tell how old he is. He could be a long, skinny twelve-year-old or a shorter, still skinny, sixteen-year-old. He's got a face like a schoolboy in a cartoon drawing: freckles across his nose the size of sultanas and a lick of carroty hair falling over his forehead. I don't even know if I can call him a friend of mine or not. I mean, he chats away the whole time we're together. In fact he never stops talking from the time I meet him till the bus comes along, and he has this funny way of speaking which isn't a bit the way most people tell you things. In spite of his chatting, though, I know almost nothing about him. I don't know where he lives or where he goes to school, and he's always on his own when I see him so I don't know who his friends are. Also, because my friends all beetle off home so quickly, they've never seen Benson, so I can't ask them if they recognize him. But, as I've said before, Benson never shuts up for a minute and what he's always on about are his relations. They seem to be a really peculiar lot, all the aunts and uncles and cousins in assorted shapes and sizes: all the in-laws, and the once-removed, the long-lost and the only-just-been-born, not to mention four grandparents, each one more astonishing than the last.

If even one tenth of what Benson says is true, then it's not the kind of family you see every day.

Last time I met him he said: 'Have I ever told you about my great-aunt Lally?'

That was a name I hadn't heard. It's not likely to have

slipped my mind. I said: 'No, I don't think you have.'

'Very stylish is my great-aunt Lally,' said Benson. 'It comes of being partly French on her mother's side. Lally's short for Eulalie and, of course, she's worked in the theatre all her life.'

'Is she an actress?'

Benson laughed. 'Oh, no ... poor little Great-Aunt Lally is far too skinny and old for that. You should try and imagine a rather well-dressed mouse . . .' (I imagined a mouse in a royal blue velvet suit with a fur hat on) '... with a very wrinkled skin and a soft voice, but an iron will. Oh, there's not much you can get away with when she's around. Beadiest old eyes in the business, Great-Aunt Lally has. Have you been imagining beady eyes?'

I nodded vigorously.

'Good, because she doesn't miss a trick.'

'But,' I interrupted him, which isn't an easy thing to do, I can tell you, 'you haven't said what she does in the theatre. All you've said is, she isn't an actress.'

'She's a dresser.'

The well-dressed, ancient, beady-eyed mouse I had been picturing disappeared out of my head. It was replaced by a piece of kitchen furniture like a cupboard with shelves above it full of plates and mugs and stuff. Benson soon put a stop to that though. It was almost as if he could read my mind. 'Not a kitchen dresser, of course, but someone who dresses the actors and makes sure all the costumes are clean before a performance and hung up neatly afterwards. Someone who stands in the wings if a person has to change clothes very quickly, and hands them all their bits and pieces in the right order and makes sure they're properly done up at the back: that's the kind of thing I mean.'

'I see,' I said. 'It sounds like fun.'

'Oh, it is,' said Benson. 'It's the most enormous fun. I know because one day I had to stand in for Great-Aunt Lally. Yes, don't look so amazed. I did, honestly. I took her place for one whole performance. It was the Saturday matinee of the pantomime, last year. The tenth of November was the date. Great-Aunt Lally had heard, you see, that Araminta Ponsonby was visiting the local bookshop and signing copies of her latest book. I can hear you thinking: Who or what is Araminta Ponsonby? And all I can say is, it's easy to see that you're not an expert on Romance. Miss Ponsonby is a writer of Romantic Novels, the kind of books to which Great-Aunt Lally is addicted. She is a gobbler-up of these books and nothing in the world would have stopped her going to the bookshop that afternoon and seeing the divine Araminta in the flesh, and buying her own personally inscribed copy of *Savage Kiss*. "Great-Aunt Lally," I told her, "I can't think why you want some totally strange woman scribbling her name all over your nice clean book ... and anyway, I could write her name, or you could, and no one would be any the wiser. You don't have to traipse all the way to the Arndale Centre."

'Great-Aunt Lally sighed and said I was too young to understand, and then she began to fret and fuss about who could take her place for the matinee. "Well, Elsie can't because she's having her palm read, and Cissy's on duty down at the Grey Parrot and I wouldn't ask Marge because she'd come over all faint from the responsibility. I suppose I could try our Brenda, but she'd go and miss all the cues, with her ears all plugged up like that. Does she ever take her Walkman off? Tell me that if you can."

' "I can't, Great-Aunt Lally," I told her. "I've never seen her without it."

' "That's that, then," said Great-Aunt Lally. "I shall have to give up seeing Araminta." She took a lace-edged hankie out of her cardigan cuff and touched the corners of her eyes.

' "What about me?" I said. "I can do it. I'm not doing anything special on Saturday afternoon."

' "You?" Great-Aunt Lally looked amazed. "How could you do it? You're only a tiddler... still, you've got a lot more sense than some, I will say that. D'you honestly think you could? I mean, there are certain problems."

'And then she told me about Chuckles "Gimme-a-baked-potato-and-a-dozen-doughnuts" Chessington, who was playing the Dame. He was the star of the show, the darling of millions, the terror of the backstage staff and anyone at all who wasn't a fan. You've probably heard of Chuckles. He was the comic sensation of the moment last year, and it was hard to open the *Radio Times* or the newspapers without reading something about him or seeing his fat, ugly mug perched on top of his fatter, uglier body. Chuckles is huge, and when I say huge, I'm not saying plump, or cuddly, or big, or portly, or well set-up, or a little on the heavy side. I'm not saying: well-muscled, thighs like treetrunks, or any of that stuff. I'm saying: GINORMOUS AND FLABBY AND SQUASHY AND WHITE AND WOBBLY and hardly able to totter round the stage.

'I listened while Great-Aunt Lally gave me a quick run-down of some of Chuckles's more endearing habits, and went white as she was speaking. There wasn't anything nasty that a person can do to another person that he wasn't busy doing. He'd reduced three stage managers to tears, he'd broken the conductor's baton over his podgy knees in a fit of temper, and he was personally responsible for four sackings and about six people in props and lighting handing in their notice. He sneered at everyone, was permanently sarcastic and only ever smiled when he was under a spotlight and being paid over the odds to do it.

' "But you should be all right," Great-Aunt Lally told me. "Tell him I'll be in directly after the matinee to get things ready for the evening, and duck very quickly if he throws that heavy glass ashtray. He does tend to do that if his beefburgers are overdone ... oh, and don't forget, you have to keep him well stocked with food.

Little bites between scenes, that's his style."

'I've got to admit to you that I was a bit nervous as I went into the theatre that day. It wouldn't be honest of me to hide that, but the thought of Great-Aunt Lally seeing her beloved Araminta Ponsonby kept me going. That, and a feeling of fascination I had about Chuckles. Well, everyone likes a close look at a monster, don't they? It's scary and exciting at the same time, know what I mean?

'Nothing Great-Aunt Lally had told me prepared me for the sight of Chuckles's dressing room. On one wall there was a mirror surrounded by light bulbs, and underneath that, a shelf where Chuckles kept his make-up. At the back of the room was a rail squeaking under the weight of the dresses Chuckles had to wear during the panto. These dresses were in bright pink, and blue and yellow, all full of beads and sequins and tinselly fringes so that they glittered and glowed and shimmered and shone and sparkled away, doing their best to liven up the room. They weren't really succeeding. Every space was covered with food: waiting to be eaten, being eaten now, having been half-eaten in the recent past. It was as though someone had taken a cake shop, a sweet shop, a pie shop, a fast-food chain and a wine merchant's, poured everything that was in them into this tiny space, given the whole thing a good mix round with a wooden spoon and then plonked Chuckles into the middle of it.

'And if the room was bad, well, you should have seen

Chuckles. I don't think anything I could tell you could convey the sight of him in his blue, army-tent-sized bathrobe: all those dunes of pasty flesh cascading from his neck down to his waist ... ugh ... I can hardly bear to think about it. And he wasn't best pleased with me, either. He started laying into me the minute he saw me, without letting me get a word in edgeways about Great-Aunt Lally or Araminta or the fact that I was only going to be here for one performance. A stream of abuse fell out of his mouth the moment I walked in. Horrible words curled out of his face and mingled with all the litter in the dressing room: half-moons of partly eaten hamburgers, pizzas on which the tomato paste had dried to a bloody crust, bricks of crumbling sponge cake.

'I shook myself and said as bravely as I could: "I think it's time we were dressing for Act One," and went to the rail to take off the blue satin creation Great-Aunt Lally had described to me.

'The matinee passed. Bad times do in the end, don't they? During the interval, Chuckles threw a cup of coffee at a poor, scared young woman who would have been badly burned if she hadn't run out of the room as though every devil in hell were behind her. Also during the interval, Chuckles summoned the drummer from the orchestra and threatened to get him sacked. The drum roll that had greeted the Dame's first entrance was, it seemed, badly timed. Me, he sent across the road (in the pouring rain, mind) for another couple of pints of brown ale, and then boxed my ears for being late back – he'd had to squeeze into his Lurex tracksuit all by himself – on and on at me he went.

'It was when he came off stage in the Lurex tracksuit that I had my brilliant idea. I wish you could have seen him: a monstrous golden slug, that's what he looked like. He waddled back into the dressing room, and by pushing and pulling together we managed to get him out of the tracksuit and into the tartan taffeta just in time for the next entrance. When he'd gone, I sat down in the dressing room for a breather and, I can tell you, I was practically exhausted just from the one show. How did Great-Aunt Lally manage, that's what I couldn't understand. I looked at the golden tracksuit hanging on the rail, and a beautiful thought came into my mind. I took a pair of scissors from Chuckles's make-up kit and, very, very delicately, began to cut a tiny stitch here, and another one there along a couple of crucial seams. It had to be done most carefully. He had to be able to get the outfit on and go on stage without anybody noticing anything ... but ... I knew that what he had to do in the tracksuit was take part in a joke exercise class. All the dancers were in their leotards around him and he had to bend and stretch and jump about and that was supposed to be funny. Well, tonight it would be a hoot. I was busy taking care of that.

'When Great-Aunt Lally came back at five o'clock clutching *Savage Kiss* to her skinny chest, I said: "I've managed all right."

'"Thank you ever so much, dear," said Great-Aunt Lally. "I don't know how I can ever repay you."

'"Can I watch the show tonight?" I asked. "I'd really love to see what it looks like from the front."

'Great-Aunt Lally couldn't imagine why I'd want to sit through two and a half hours of Chuckles at his creepiest, but I had to know if my trick had worked.

'I hardly noticed the first act at all. I was waiting for the exercise class scene. When Chuckles appeared in the Lurex, I could hardly breathe properly. As the music started for the dance, I was on the edge of my seat, waiting. There he was: bend, stretch, bend, stretch, twist ... oh, my, wasn't it going to work? Would the Lurex never give? Then, all at once, there was a ripping sound so loud that it crackled across the music, and the seams at the back of the tracksuit tore along their whole length, and there was Chuckles's enormous, flabby bum (in knickers, it's true, but still an enormous bum) lit by thirty separate beams of light for everyone to see. The laughter that greeted this astounding sight was enormous, deafening, overwhelming. Chuckles turned so that his back was away from the audience, and the seams around his arms tore noisily and rolls of flesh began erupting from unexpected openings in the golden cloth.

'He was red in the face with embarrassment. The dancers had stopped dancing, they were so helpless with laughter. Chuckles tottered across the stage in his ruined suit with the whole audience whistling and catcalling and yelling: "Take it off! Take it off!" The curtain came down after that, and a white-faced man in evening dress whispered into a microphone that tonight's performance had been cancelled, owing to Chuckles's indisposition.

'Great-Aunt Lally told me later that "our fat friend", as she called him, had left the show for good shortly afterwards, and gone to sulk in his penthouse and console himself by tunnelling through mountain ranges of food and draining rivers of booze. His part as Dame was taken by Bubbles Gillespie, who was a great success all round and deeply beloved by the entire company. Isn't this your bus coming?'

'Yes, it is,' I said. 'Will you be here tomorrow?'

'P'raps,' Benson said. 'P'raps not. Remind me to tell you about the time my uncle Paddy got his foot stuck in a teapot.'

I jumped on to the bus and waved until Benson was out of sight.

Doctor BB

by Susan Kajura
(UGANDA)

illustrated by Catherine Anholt

It was around dusk when Doctor BB arrived in Kauka village. He wore a black coat, white robe and, carried an hat and umbrella, and was perched bird-like on the back of a motorcycle. He rented a room behind Hajati's shop and that's where he opened his clinic.

'Doctor for everything,' Hajati told her customers. 'Coughs, colds and fever, you name it.' Then she whispered, 'He can even tell you why you have no money.'

'I know why I have no money; where to find it is the problem,' Ponsiano laughed. He hated work and liked to hang around shops.

'If he's told you where to find money, tell us!' Muko shouted excitedly. He was thirteen years old and should not have been in Hajati's store on a weekday afternoon.

'Get back to class, Muko Mulondo, school is not over yet!' Hajati scolded.

'My mama sent me here, she's sick, she needs a handkerchief. A handkerchief from your well-stocked shop.'

Hajati thought Muko might be lying, about his mother being sick that is, but no one could dispute his other statement: her shop was indeed well stocked. In fact the best-stocked shop in Kauka. Hajati's shop had everything: groceries, cutlery, lanterns and cups. Buckets, basins, underwear and every brand of handcream you could imagine. Her merchandise hung from hooks on the walls or was piled high in a colourful mixture on the shelves. Sacks of sugar, rice, flour and beans stood haphazardly in front of the shop counter.

'What has Doctor BB done for you?' Ponsiano asked.

'Helped me with my chickens,' Hajati whispered. 'They had stopped laying, you know. He told me exactly what to do, and bang, just like that, there were eggs everywhere!'

'That's amazing.'

'My mother has two cockerels; can he make them lay eggs?' Muko shouted. Muko wasn't supposed to have heard what Hajati said.

'Can you pay for your handkerchief and go!' Hajati snapped. One hand was on her hip, and the other was outstretched for payment.

'Mama will send the money tomorrow,' Muko replied sheepishly, which only confirmed Hajati's suspicions. But just in case he was telling the truth she said, 'Then tomorrow's when you will get your handkerchief. Goodbye.' Hajati squeezed her plump shape from behind the counter and marched Muko's lanky frame out of her shop.

'He needs your Doctor BB to help him know when he's being a nuisance,' Ponsiano laughed.

'He needs Doctor BB to help him pass his exams, more like. Do you know that he is only in Standard Four? Thirteen years old and only in Standard Four. He is now in the same form with his younger sister, Nalu. Mark my words, he won't pass the end-of-year exams either. You know what's going to happen to him?'

'What?' Ponsiano was all ears; so was Muko, who was listening outside.

'His younger sister will pass him and move on to Standard Five, and his little brother Samsoni, who is now in Standard One, will eventually find him and do the same.' Hajati laughed her hiccup laugh and was joined by Ponsiano, who snorted like a pig.

Muko was really hurt and he slouched off home. *Hajati is wrong,* he thought, *and I am going to show her. I am going to show everybody in Kauka who laughs at me.*

As he approached his house Muko remembered he had to hide and wait for four o'clock. Hajati had been right about one thing concerning Muko: the boy was skipping school again.

'You missed your first exam this afternoon!' his sister announced when Muko came in. Nine-year-old Nalu was doing her revision at the dining-room table. For blurting out his secret, Muko cuffed her ear.

'Mamaaa.' Nalu left the table and Muko heard her

whiny voice telling on him. He waited for the kitchen door to fling open, which it did.

'Muko, why have you done this? Why have you done this?' Mrs Mulondo wagged her finger.

'And I didn't even do anything to him!' Nalu wailed.

'Muko, I am tired of you hurting my children. You are the eldest, you should be the one protecting and not hurting them.'

'He left school at lunchtime!'

'That's it! Go to your room and wait for your father.'

Muko lay on his bed with his hands behind his head, staring up at the ceiling. He was thinking about what to do. His father had warned him, any more complaints and he should prepare for the 'caning of a lifetime'. 'DON'T YOU KNOW ANYTHING, BOY?' his father had shouted.

Knowledge, Muko thought, that was his problem, really. That was the reason he couldn't understand anything in school. The reason Nalu had caught up with him and the reason little Samsoni threatened to do the same. Muko didn't 'KNOW ANYTHING!' To make matters worse, the end-of-year exams had started and he'd already failed the one he'd missed, maths. When Muko turned to face the wall, an idea came to him. *If Doctor BB can make hens lay eggs, surely he can help me pass exams! I must go to him before Dad gets back.*

Muko jumped off his bed and peeped round his

bedroom door. There was no one in the corridor. Muko could hear Nalu's whiny voice reciting some formulae to Mama in the sitting room. He slipped out of the front door and crossed the yard to the gate.

'Get back to your room!' Mrs Mulondo popped her head out of the window.

Muko thought quickly.

'I need to collect Dad's jacket from the Dobbie man.'

'Hmm, it was due today. Well, hurry back. If you find it's not yet ready, leave it, don't wait for it, come straight back.'

Muko skipped out of the gate and ran all the way back to the shops.

Doctor BB's clinic was in the courtyard behind Hajati's store. Muko walked across the yard's cobbled ground and stopped at an open doorway with the words 'BB the Healer' written over the top.

Two wooden benches had been placed outside the door. Papyrus mats covered the floor inside and two massive sheets of bark cloth stretched across the room. They hung like curtains from the ceiling to the floor.

'Take your shoes off when you step into the house of the healer.' A voice made Muko jump. It came from the far side of the bark cloth. Muko took off his sandals and entered. He sat down cross-legged on a mat just inside the doorway with his back against the wall.

'Your name?'

'Muko.'

'Ah, Muko Mulondo,' the voice said and made Muko jump a second time.

'I know what brings you here.'

'You do?'

'Your exams.'

Muko shook in excitement.

'Then you can help me?'

'What exam do you have tomorrow?'

'Science.'

'Ah, you will need the *Book of Knowledge One*, together with the Magic Bead and Herbs of Wisdom.

Muko was beside himself.

'You have them!' he cried.

'Yes, I have them, but whether they will be of any help will depend on you.' The voice paused. 'And your willingness to follow my instructions.'

Muko's heart quickened.

'I will, I will,' he gasped.

'Good. Now listen carefully. Everything you are about to hear must stay in this room. Promise.'

'Promise!'

'Tonight, you must take supper early. If you are offered meat, refuse it. In your pocket you will have the Magic Bead and Herbs of Wisdom. Against your skin you will carry the *Book of Knowledge One*. After you have eaten, go to an empty room and wait for the signal. The night owl will hoot three times. At that moment open the book and place the bead on your head. Start to read the secret of how the universe works. You will read of magnetic fields and electricity, how plants grow and humans fight disease.'

'I want to know all that!' Muko rubbed his hands.

'By the time you have finished the book,' the voice continued, 'you will have gained knowledge on all that and much more, because the powers of the night will have pushed the words you are reading through the bead into your head. It's only the words you read that will enter the bead, so take care you don't miss a thing.' Muko nodded eagerly.

'You will read and read until you hear the Full Moon Howl. As soon as you hear it, close your book and go to sleep. Knowledge uses sleeptime to settle down inside you. In the morning you will stir that knowledge by bathing with the Herbs of Wisdom. Put back the bead on your head during exams, it will bring the knowledge up and you can use it to answer exam questions.'

'Give me the book, the bead, the herbs, everything!' Muko shouted.

'You will get them all shortly, once you have paid.'

'Paid!'

'Did you not intend to pay, Muko?'

'Yes, I mean no, of course I intended to p-p-pay. My dad's a taxi driver. H-h-h-he comes with money h-h-home every day. He will pay.'

'How can I be sure? You must give me something now.'

Muko shifted uneasily. His hand brushed against a paper bag. Of course – the jacket he had collected from the Dobbie man!

'Here, Dad gave me this to give to you; it's his best jacket, worth more than money even.'

A clenched fist was thrust through the parting where the two sheets of bark cloth joined. Muko hooked the jacket on to the waiting fist. The jacket got pulled in. A hand re-emerged with two little packages of banana leaves. Muko grabbed them, and then took the book that was handed to him when the hand came out a third time. On the bark-cloth cover of the book were the words *Book of Knowledge One*.

'Go well, Muko, and remember my instructions. I shall see you this time tomorrow.'

Muko could barely keep himself from tripping as he hurried home.

His behaviour that evening earned him his mother's forgiveness.

'Husband, you should have seen him,' she said to Mr Mulondo when he got home. 'Muko ate early and went straight to his room to revise for tomorrow's science exam.'

'How long do you think he will keep that up!' Mr Mulondo frowned.

'I don't know,' his wife snapped. She thought Mr Mulondo should have sounded pleased with Muko's effort. 'If our beloved son is trying to become good, we should support him, dear husband.'

'Whatever you say, dear wife. Just make sure he remembers to collect my shoes from the cobbler when he returns from school tomorrow.'

On the way to school the next morning, Muko smelt funny.

'He bathed with herbs you know,' little Samsoni whispered to his sister.

During exams that afternoon Nalu watched her brother write with a bead on his head. The rest of the class sniggered into their papers.

'Muko was acting strange, Mum!' Nalu said when they got back from school.

'As long as he's trying.' Mrs Mulondo smiled and she reminded her son to collect his father's shoes from the cobbler.

'I will go now,' Muko said, 'and if they are not ready, I won't wait for them, I shall collect them on another day.' Mrs Mulondo was so pleased to hear him say something so sensible.

That evening Muko had an early supper and retired to his room to read again. He had come back from the 'cobbler' with the *Book of Knowledge Two*. It told of valleys, mountains and lakes, and he read it until a dog howled at the moon outside. By morning Muko was ready for his geography exam.

On the third evening, Muko returned from a visit to the 'tailor' with the *Book of Knowledge Three* tucked inside his shirt.

'Were your dad's trousers ready?' Mum asked.

'No, and I couldn't wait for them because I want to study for tomorrow's history exam.'

His mother beamed as she watched her son enter his bedroom.

Muko waited for the owl's signal, then he put the bead on his head and became so engrossed in the legends he was reading, he almost missed the commotion outside the house.

Mr Mulondo's taxi was hooting at the gate.

'Open up!' he cried. He revved the engine as he drove the minibus in. He stopped right in front of the main entrance and jumped out. Mr Mulondo slammed the car door and marched over to the passenger side, where he dragged out a waif-like man in huge jacket, flowing trousers, and shoes that were several sizes too big.

'This man has stolen my clothes, Safia!' he shouted to his wife. 'He got into my taxi wearing *my* jacket, *my* shoes, *my* trousers. What is this?'

'Where did you get my husband's clothes?' Mrs Mulondo gasped as she came bustling outside.

The waif-like man slipped out of Mr Mulondo's grasp and smoothed down his clothes, and with what dignity he could muster, he said in a surprisingly deep voice, 'Madam, these clothes are mine. They were given to me by your son, Muko. I am his healer, Doctor BB.'

'What?' the Mulondo parents exclaimed in unison.

'Muko came to me sick of school and afraid of exams. In exchange for these clothes, which he said were from you, I taught him how to read for knowledge, which he used in his exams.'

'I never sent Muko to you with my clothes!' Mr Mulondo shouted.

'Dad, I c-c-can explain.' Muko had crept up to the doorway. 'I had no m-money and I n-needed his help. I was going to find w-w-work in the holidays. B-b-b-bring him money and g-get b-back your clothes.'

'Prepare for the caning of a lifetime. DON'T YOU KNOW ANYTHING, BOY?' Mr Mulondo roared.

'Dad, Muko passed science today; our teacher was very excited!' Nalu whispered.

'Indeed, he will pass them all!' the doctor said. 'The boy has found books that speak to him. I gave him books that dealt with the same topics he was learning in school, the difference being my books presented them in a way he could understand.'

'That doesn't excuse him giving my clothes away,' Mr Mulondo snarled.

'No, dear husband, but perhaps we can work something out with the good doctor. He can give us the clothes back and let Muko work in the holidays to pay him.'

As Mrs Mulondo said this Muko nodded vigorously.

'Under the circumstances, I have no option but to agree.' The doctor straightened his jacket. 'Muko can work for me – sweep my clinic and run a few errands over the holidays. In fact, he can start today, by returning the clothes and shoes back to his father.'

'Thank you,' Muko sighed.

'Yes, thank you, Doctor BB. But before you go, please join us for supper.' Mrs Mulondo smiled. 'And maybe over dinner you can tell us what "BB" stands for.'

'I bet it's Beads and Books!' Samsoni cried.

'No, it's Boys' Brains,' Nalu teased, and Muko showed her his fist.

'Now, now,' Mrs Mulondo laughed. 'We shall let the good doctor tell us over tonight's supper of chicken and rice.'

'Chicken and rice!' the children cried, and turned and raced each other inside.

'Muko's already eaten!' Nalu shouted.

'Who said?' Muko snarled.

Everyone laughed as they all went in to eat.

A Dog Called John

by Karen McCombie

(UNITED KINGDOM)

illustrated by Lindsey Gardiner

'What's he barking at, Ellie?' my friend Sara asked, the first time she met John.

'The fridge,' I replied wearily.

'Why?' Sara frowned, slapping her hands on either side of her head to protect her eardrums from the racket.

'He doesn't like it,' I shrugged.

In the three days we'd had him, we'd found out that John didn't like a *lot* of things. Apart from the fridge, he seemed to have a grudge against the beanbag, the chest of drawers in the hall, and he *definitely* wasn't too fond of the wicker laundry basket.

'He's weird,' Sara mumbled, backing away from him.

'I know,' I nodded, wondering what I'd got myself into.

Course, it was my own fault – I'd wanted a dog, I always had. If you'd looked back in my diary for this year, you'd have seen tons of entries like: *Went to Nan's house. Ate so much cake I felt sick. Please let me have a dog,* and *Darren Smith did a huge burp in class today. Too much homework. Please let me have a dog.*

But it wasn't that simple. I didn't want *any* old dog; I wanted the sort of dog that's smart, the sort of dog that made the front page of the local paper for bringing you a bar of chocolate when you were slipping into a diabetic coma, or that saved small children from shark-infested waters by dragging them out by their nappies before human help arrived.

OK, so I didn't have diabetes (and, strictly speaking, I'm not sure if you're meant to *eat* or *avoid* chocolate if you're slipping into a diabetic coma). And, OK, so there aren't any shark-infested waters round where I live, but you get the idea. I just wanted the sort of dog I could be the proud owner of at *The Animal Awards* on the telly, where famous people would shake me by the hand and wipe tears from their eyes as they listened to tales of my dog's courage.

But instead of a smart, courageous dog, I got John.

John the dog.

John the dog, who looked like a very small, round barrel on legs, and whose hobbies were barking at furniture and sleeping with his tongue lolling out.

John the dog, named 'John' by his former owner, called (wait for this) *John*, who happened to be my nan's elderly next-door neighbour, but who'd gone and died and left his namesake without a home.

And not long after I got John, instead of a diary, I ended up with enough chewed, soggy paper to take up papier mâché as a hobby.

'Well, you *did* say you wanted a dog, didn't you, Ellie?'

my mum pointed out to me in that ever-so-patronizing way she does sometimes, when she likes to remind me that I'm eleven and technically still a kid (gee, thanks *very* much). 'And we can always get you another diary.'

The thing was, I know it was only a bunch of pages inside a cardboard cover, but I thought Mum would have understood why it mattered so much to me. After all, *she* was the one who bought me it, after I'd finished *The Diary of Anne Frank* – the first book I'd ever read the whole way through and loved without having my arm twisted into it at school. 'You see?' she'd said to me at the time, thrilled that I'd finally found a book that didn't bore me so much I wanted to chuck it at a wall. 'It's just a case of finding out what type of books interest you, that's all.'

Well, the type of book that turned out to interest me was anything to do with true-life stories and, as soon as I got my own diary, I started telling my own true-life story – even if it *was* pretty dull at times.

And yeah, so some days I didn't write too much in it, but other days I scribbled on and on, pouring out all my problems to it like it was some silent best friend. I wrote in that book for two-thirds of a year, and then John ate it in two minutes. I left him sprawled and snoring on my bedroom floor for two *tiny* minutes while I went to the loo, and when I came back, he was that bit fatter and my life was that bit emptier.

So that's John – the most useless dog in the world.

And I haven't even *started* on the most useless brother in the world...

I might not have been too thrilled about the dog I ended up with, but at least it was my choice to have one. I didn't have *any* choice about having a brother.

I just got born and there he was, three years old and already nicking things from me. My nan's got this photo of me in my buggy clutching a rusk, while my brother – whose mouth is covered with the evidence of the chocolate biscuit he's just scoffed – is trying to prise it from my chubby fingers without realizing my parents have spotted him. 'Course, Mum and Dad let him get away with it, thinking it was adorably funny, just like they think *everything* about Dylan is adorably funny.

From then on, as far as Dylan was concerned, having a little sister around was like having a never-ending source of emergency supplies. Finished his tea and still hungry? He could nab that sausage off my plate! All his Plasticine got mushed together into one boring brown lump? He could help himself to my brand new, multicoloured pack! Left the tops off all his felt-tip pens? He could start leaving the tops off mine and dry *them* out too!

And, of course, once Dylan realized that I didn't blow all my pocket money within an hour of getting it (like, er, *him*), he started borrowing *that* from me too. Honestly, sometimes I feel like an eleven-year-old bank manager.

So how come I let Dylan get away with it? Well, I guess because a) he's my big brother, and b) he's got this annoyingly funny way of charming you. You want an example? Well, take today after school…

I'd been trying to take John for a drag around the park, but we'd only got as far as the waste ground at the end of the road when he parked his bum on the pavement and refused to go any further. (He does this a lot. Apparently, the closest he got to exercise with his old owner was watching cricket on TV while sharing a bag of Werther's Originals.)

Luckily for me, there was a bunch of boys roaring around with a football on the patchy grass of the waste ground, so at least I could pretend to be vaguely interested in their game. Normally, when John does this stubborn sitting-down thing, I think that people just assume I'm some demented person staring into space with only a small barrel attached by a long bit of string for company.

'Hey, Slasher!' Dylan suddenly called out, appearing muddily from the throng of lads thundering around.

'What's the point in calling him that?' I asked Dylan as he jogged closer. I didn't have to look down at John to know he'd not flickered so much as the tip of an ear at the sound of Dylan's yell. It didn't matter how much my brother wanted our – *my* – new dog to have a tough name, the only thing he'd answer to was John. That, or 'Here, boy – toffee!'

'He could get used to it!' Dylan beamed, reaching over and scratching John on the head. *That* got a reaction all right: John turned his dark, dopey eyes in Dylan's direction and smiled at him. Or maybe it was a sneer, or even a half-hearted snarl ... it was hard to tell what went on inside his doggy brain.

Anyway, why should John like the nickname Dylan had given him, when I didn't like the one he'd given me?

'Is that my bag?' I asked, suddenly spotting the black nylon Nike rucksack that was currently being used as a goal post.

'Oh, that? Yeah,' Dylan nodded, an infuriating grin on his face. 'You don't mind, do you, Smellie? Mine was covered in mud from school yesterday.'

And now mine was going to be covered in mud *too*.

Before I got the chance to moan, Dylan slapped an arm around me and spun round in the direction of his mates, yelling, 'Hey, did I tell you my little sister is the coolest little sister in the world?'

See what I mean about cranking up the charm?

None of the guys looked particularly impressed, but as Dylan is the unofficial leader of their unofficial gang, they were hardly going to argue with him, even if the red-faced kid with the barrel on the end of the string was just about as far away from cool as it was possible to *get*.

'Um, listen, Smellie ... ' Dylan suddenly began, dropping his voice and turning the full force of his winning grin on me.

Uh-oh ... he was on the scrounge for something (*else*, I mean).

'No,' I told him, before I even heard what it was. So far

this week, he'd eaten my pizza when I was out of the room answering a phone call from Sara, used up the last of my favourite apple-scented shampoo, 'borrowed' fifty pence for his bus fare because he'd spent all his on a Big Mac Meal Deal after bunking off school dinners with his mate Luke, and now he'd taken my bag without even asking.

'Aw, come on, Smellie, please!' he pleaded, tilting his head to one side. 'I just need a fiver till I get my pocket money! I know it's a lot, but it's just till Saturday!'

A fiver? Who was he kidding? Did Dylan think I was a *total* mug?

It's very hard to keep a diary when your dog's just eaten it, I scribble on a blank sheet of A4 paper from my dad's printer. *And it's very hard to save up for your brother's birthday present when he keeps nicking money from you ...*

Of course I'd given in to Dylan, *again*.

'What's it for?' I'd asked him earlier, reluctantly pulling the blue note out of my tin money box.

'Just stuff,' he'd shrugged. 'Couple of us are going into town, 'cause it's late-night shopping.'

Yeah, late-night hanging out in the games arcade, more like. Well, it was his loss. If he didn't give me the money back by Saturday, all he'd be getting for his fifteenth birthday next week was a gift-wrapped packet of Wotsits.

'Writing your diary?' asks Dad, hovering at my slightly open bedroom door.

It's nearly seven o'clock. He's just got changed out of

his work clothes and will be going downstairs to watch the Channel 4 News; the first of six zillion news programmes he'll watch tonight. I think my dad is seriously addicted to news, just like my mum is seriously addicted to reading (books, magazines, newspapers, the backs of tins of beans . . .). Hey, maybe addiction runs in our family! After all, Dylan is addicted to everything of *mine*. And what am *I* addicted to? Well, it used to be keeping a diary, which is why I can't quite give it up, even if I don't have an actual *diary* any more.

'Kind of,' I reply, fidgeting with the sheet of paper.

'Oh. Right.' Dad tries to look sympathetic for like a nanosecond. 'Well, er, anyway, Mum says Dylan's gone into town. What's he gone there for?'

You know something? Mum and Dad are always more interested in Dylan than me. Right now, they're more interested in what Gameboy games Dylan's drooling over than how I feel about my diary being eaten.

'Dunno,' I shrug, suddenly feeling mad at my brother. *And* my dad. *And* my mum. *And* my stupid, useless, diary-destroying dog.

Speaking of stupid, useless, diary-destroying dogs . . .

'What about John? Where's he?' asks Dad, still hovering.

'Dunno,' I white-lie, in the hope that my dad will leave me alone and go and watch his boring old news programme instead.

'Well, I'll leave you to it, then,' he says, giving up on me and pulling my door closed behind him.

Good – I'm in the mood to be by myself, even if that mood happens to be a *bad* one.

All I am to this family is someone to borrow stuff from and look after a dumb dog who's as thick as a brick and not quite as cute, I write in a black-ink scrawl.

Somewhere under my bed, John starts snoring, exhausted after his pre-tea snack of one of my trainer socks. But then he stops with a startled snuffle, as someone taps loudly at my bedroom door.

'What?' I call out, knowing I sound like a complete grump-bucket, but I just can't help myself.

'Er … Smellie? Is it all right if we come in?'

I don't know why Dylan has even bothered to ask, seeing as he's in my room already, back from town and trailing his mate Luke with him. What's up? Has Luke heard I'm a soft touch and come to permanently borrow my Walkman or something?

Dylan is doing his grinning thing, but I'm not falling for it this time, whatever it is he wants.

'Listen, I told Luke about Slasher eating your diary,' he begins.

Oh, great. Bet they had a *right* laugh at that. I check Luke's face for signs of full-on sniggering, but there's only a medium-sized smile.

'So?' I shrug.

(Out of the corner of my eye, I see John wriggling his fat barrel belly out from under the bed – with a struggle.)

'So, he wants to write about it for the school magazine.

And take a picture.'

As Dylan speaks, Luke holds up a flashy digital camera.

'Me? In your school magazine?' I squeak, feeling my cheeks go on fire.

'Yeah, you and Slasher,' says Dylan matter-of-factly, scooping my fat dog off the floor and depositing him in my arms.

'I'll just take a couple of photos, and then I'll do an interview with you, if that's OK,' says Luke, weaving backwards and forwards as he tries to figure out the best angle to snap me.

I don't even have time to think before the first flash goes off, blinding me. John doesn't seem too sure about what's going on either, and is wriggling his fat warm belly in my arms.

'Hold on – I'll try one looking down on you,' Luke announces, dragging across the wheelie chair that lives by my desk.

'Oh, and I nearly forgot – got you a present,' Dylan grins, stepping forward and handing me a square-ish something in a paper bag.

'A present? But it's nearly *your* birthday, not *mine*!'

'Whatever,' Dylan shrugs easily, watching as I struggle to juggle wriggly John and tear the paper bag open at the same time.

It's ... it's a diary.

It's purple pretend leather with a real daisy on the front, squashed flat underneath a tiny panel of see-through plastic. It's got a minuscule silver lock on it too, with an itsy-bitsy key sticking out of it.

It's about a million miles nicer than my old diary. I don't know what to say, so I don't say anything, I just stare at it.

'I knew you were really gutted at Slasher eating your last one, so I thought I'd surprise you!' Dylan beams. 'Hope it's OK – I thought it looked like it was the sort of stuff Slasher wouldn't fancy chewing on so much.'

True. John is sniffing at the diary, but isn't even giving it a trial nibble.

'Listen, Smellie, I know I bought it with your money,' says Dylan hastily, obviously thinking that my stunned silence means something else, 'but I will pay you back!'

'Look, can you get that book thing out of shot?' Luke suddenly orders my brother, as he stands towering over me from the chair he's just clambered up on. 'And can you cuddle Slasher a bit closer, Smel– I mean, Ellie?'

I'm still so stunned by Dylan's lovely, amazing, thoughtful prezzie that I do as I'm told, and hug John to my chest.

And then the funniest thing happens: my very thick dog turns his whiskered face up to mine and stares straight at me, like he's recognizing me for the very first time.

'Hello,' I say softly, wondering if it's finally sunk into his not-very-bright-but-quite-cute head that *this* is his home, that *I've* taken over from the Werther's Originals man.

It must have done, 'cause I can feel his short sturdy tail begin whapping happily on my side, and – best of all – he starts licking my face.

'Arghh!' I can't help giggling and squirming, as the camera flash goes pinging.

'Yeah, that's good!' I hear Luke calling to me. 'But could you just try getting Slasher to look straight up at me now?'

'His name's *John*,' I set Luke straight, as I'm bombarded with happy licks again.

You'll never guess — me and John are getting our story in a magazine! That's the first thing I'm going to write in my brand-new diary, I decide in my head, blinking some more at the camera flash.

So maybe, *instead* of being super-smart, my dog happens to be super-*stupid*, and pretty cute with it. So what? And maybe John'll still end up on telly, only not on *The Animal Awards*, but on *The World's Funniest Animals* — if we manage to film him next time he's going demented at the fridge or eating the *Yellow Pages* or something.

As for my brother ... well, maybe he's not so bad either.

'Hey, Smellie, I was just thinking,' Dylan butts into my thoughts. 'That fiver ... Could I pay you back a *week* on Saturday instead? It's just that there's this CD single I really want and —'

As he witters on, I wonder if — instead of the fridge — I could train John to bark at Dylan every time he starts doing my head in ...